CONSTRUCTING WALKING JAZZ

BUILDING A 12 KEY FACILITY FOR THE JAZZ BASSIST

Book I

Upright
&
Electric Bass
Edition

By Steven Mooney

©Waterfall Publishing House 2012

This book is dedicated to my wife Madoka and my son James Omega Mooney
Special thanks to Jimmy Vass, Darcy Wright and Charlie Banacos.

Inspiration for the book comes from the following words.

" there again, get those things down in all 12 keys "

Darcy Wright.

Copyright © WATERFALL PUBLISHING HOUSE 2012

All Rights Reserved
No part of this publication may be produced, stored in a retrieval system or transmitted in any form or means , photocopying , mechanical or electronic without prior written permission of Waterfall Publishing House.

Print Edition ISBN 978-1-937187-20-0
eBook ISBN 978-1-937187-25-5
BassTab Edition ISBN 978-1-937187-23-1
eBook Bass Tab Edition ISBN 978-1-937187-27-9
Japanese Edition ISBN 978-1-937187-29-3
Japanese Bass Tab edition ISBN 978-1-937187-31-6

Library of Congress Control Number : 2012939835

Musical Score : Jazz
Musical Score : Studies & exercises, etudes

Layout and music engraving by Steven Mooney
Cover Design by Steven Mooney

Table of Contents

©Waterfall Publishing House 2012

Table of contents cont...

©Waterfall Publishing House 2012

Foreward

Building a 12 Key Facility for the Jazz Bassist is the 4th installment in the Constructing Walking Jazz Bass Lines series, and is a II part series.

Book I Building a 12 key Facility for the Jazz Bassist breaks down the jazz bass vocabulary by outlining key areas of harmonic structure related to the jazz standard and bebop styles.

As in the earlier books in the series the lesson material builds in a stepwise manner enabling the student to build on the solid foundational material discussed in books I - III.

All lessons are applied to all 12 keys with written out bass lines and MP3 backing tracks applied to 10 jazz and bebop standard chord progressions with over 150 choruses of written out bass line examples.

By practicing the material presented in this book, Book I of the series the bassist builds technical facility and expands on their jazz vocabulary by practicing the key harmonic structures used most often by jazz bassists in the jazz standard and bebop styles.

Presented in this book and outlined with written out examples in all 12 keys are the fundamentals required by the professional jazz bassist.

The II V I in major modulating to II V I in minor
Voice Leading
The I VI II V over 2 and 4 measures
The I VI II V progression and the secondary dominant chord
The V of V cycle
The I IV III VI progression
The bVII Dominant 7th chord & the IV Minor bVII7 progression
The IV Minor bVII7 progression
The IV Major to IV Minor bVII7 progression
Turnarounds into the II IV & VI chords
Diatonic chord structures & the II V into the IV chord Bridge
Tritone substitution
Tritone substitution chord progressions
Accents, phrasing & anticipating the chord changes
The Minor key tonality & the Minor II V progression
The descending Minor II V I Bridge
Tritone substitution of the Altered dominant chord.

Building a 12 Key Facility for the Jazz Bassist Book II is dedicated specifically to chord and scale studies in 12 keys.
Featuring major scale studies and modes, minor scale studies, diminished, whole tone and augmented scales.
With written out examples of how to practice the scales, chords and modes in all 12 keys.

©Waterfall Publishing House 2012

Download the Playalong backing tracks to this book and other books in the Constructing Walking Jazz Bass Lines Series at http://constructingwalkingjazzbasslines.com/playalong-downloads.html

©Waterfall Publishing House 2012

Chapter 1 VOICE LEADING 7th CHORDS & THE MAJOR II V I PROGRESSION IN 12 KEYS

The following chapter outlines the voice leading technique and how it is applied to constructing walking jazz bass lines. Examples are outlined in all 12 keys.

The voice leading technique will be used to link the IImin7 chord to the V7 chord. Voice leading is a very effective technique used by all harmonic instruments.
By using the voice leading technique shown below the bass lines are now connected to how the pianist or guitarist may voice the chords.

Ex. 1 shows the chart of the diatonic 7th chords in the key of G major. *

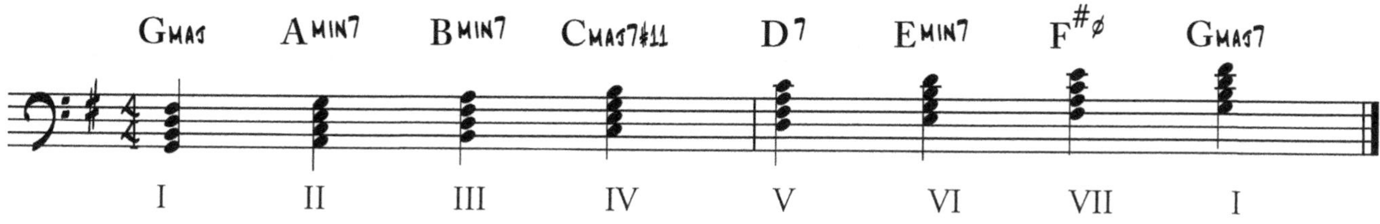

Ex. 2 shows the II V I progression in the key of G major using a walking bass line with no voice leading on the II V progression.

Ex. 3 shows the II V I progression in the key of G major using a walking bass line incorporating the voice leading technique, here the G the b7th of Amin7 resolves down a half step to the F# the major 3rd of D7.

The voice leading notes are highlighted with brackets on all examples.

* Constructing the diatonic 7th chords has been discussed in greater detail in Book III of the Constructing Walking Jazz Bass Lines series - Standard Lines.

©Waterfall Publishing House 2012

Ex. 4 shows the II V I progression in the key of G major using a walking bass line incorporating the voice leading technique, here the G the b7th of Amin7 resolves up a whole step to the A the 5th of D7.

Amin7
D7
Gmaj7
II
V
I

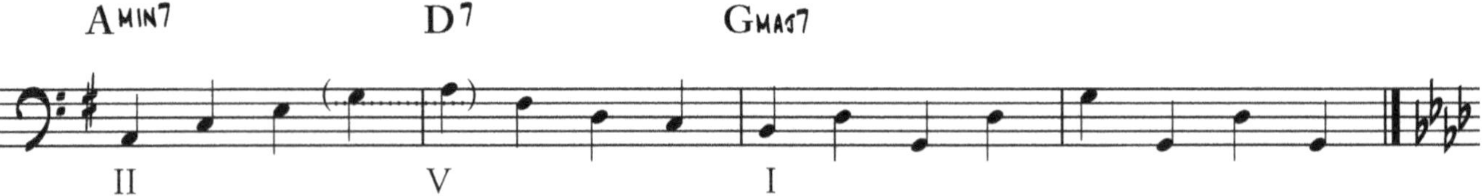

Continued below are the voice leading examples applied to the Major II V I progression in the remaining keys.

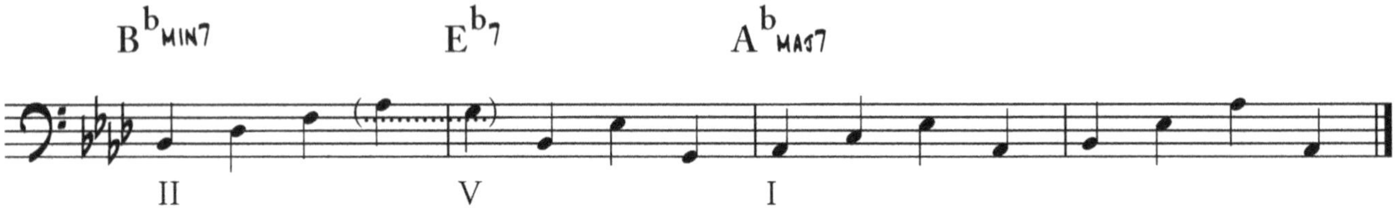
Bbmin7
Eb7
Abmaj7
II
V
I

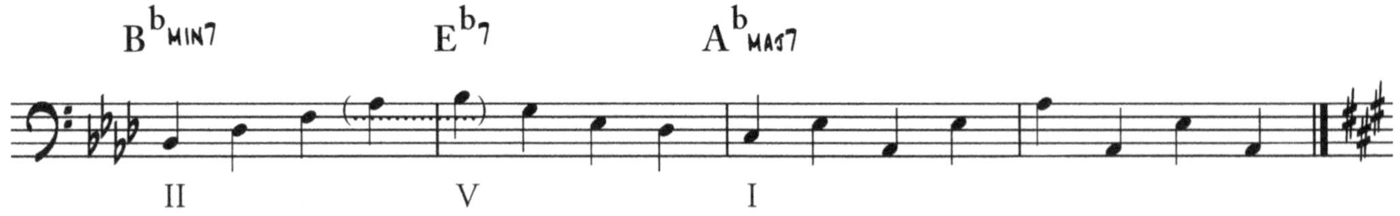
Bbmin7
Eb7
Abmaj7
II
V
I

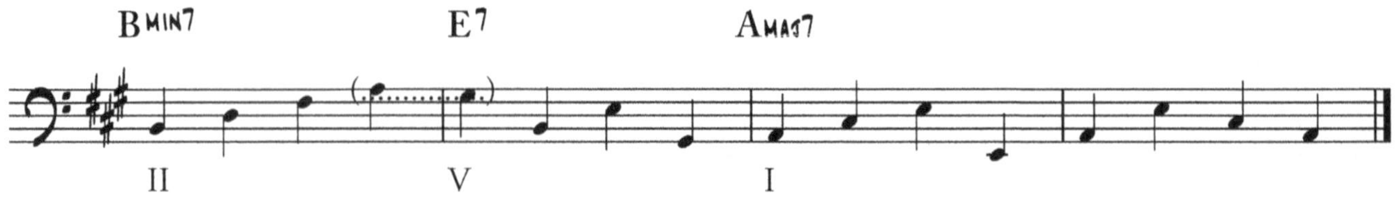
Bmin7
E7
Amaj7
II
V
I

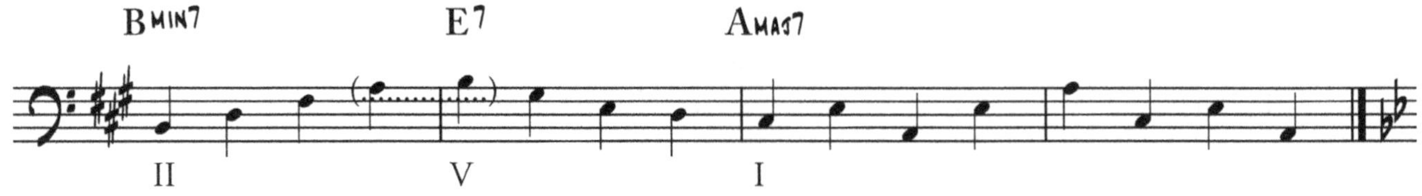
Bmin7
E7
Amaj7
II
V
I

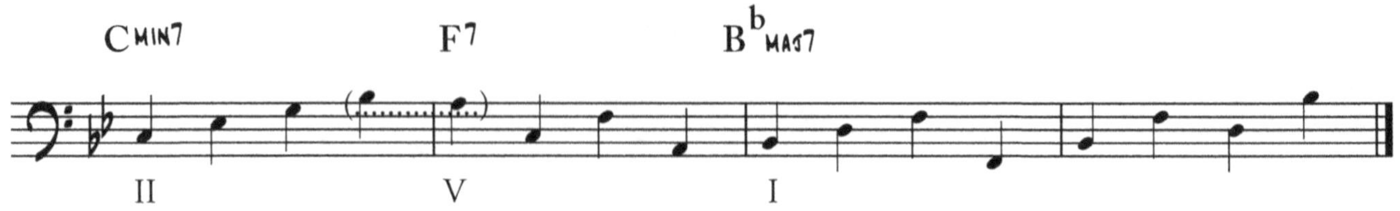
Cmin7
F7
Bbmaj7
II
V
I

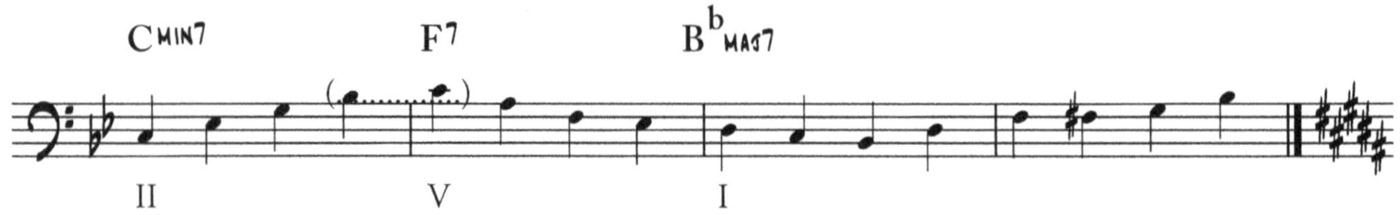
Cmin7
F7
Bbmaj7
II
V
I

©Waterfall Publishing House 2012

©Waterfall Publishing House 2012

©Waterfall Publishing House 2012

Chapter 2. The II V I IN MAJOR MODULATING TO II V I INTO THE RELATIVE MINOR

Jazz chord progression #1 outlines the classic jazz standard harmonic progression of the II V I in Major modulating to the II V I into the Relative Minor and incorporates the voice leading technique outlined in chapter 1.
Example 1 outlines the relationship of the Major and Relative Minor chords using the diatonic 7ths chart in the key of G Major.
In the key of G Major the I Major chord is G maj7 and the Relative Minor chord is the VI chord E min7.

Ex. 1

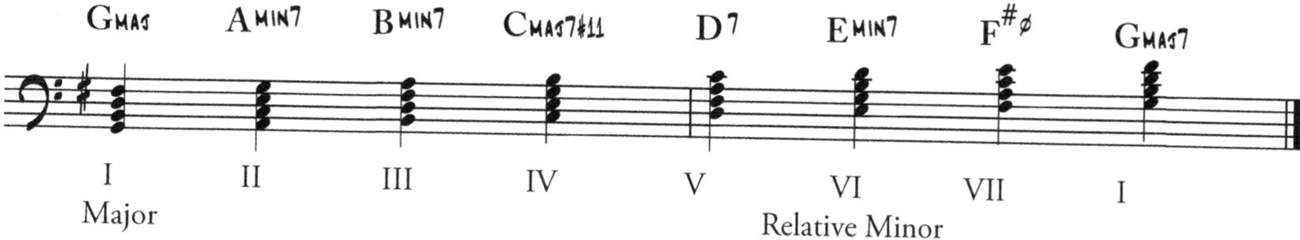

Ex. 2 The II V I progression in G Major

Ex. 3 The II V I of the Relative Minor E Minor

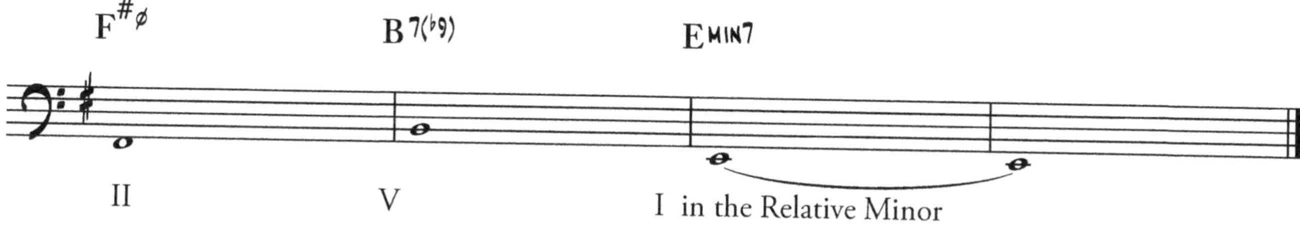

©Waterfall Publishing House 2012

Ex. 4 JAZZ STANDARD CHORD PROGRESSION #1 IN DIGITAL FORM

©Waterfall Publishing House 2012

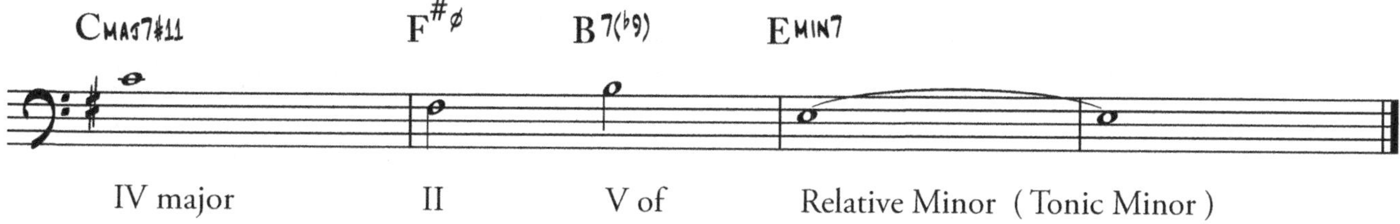

Jazz chord progression #1 is written in a minor key. eg Emin7

Ex. 5 The first 8 measures of Jazz chord progression # 1

ANALIZING THE FIRST 8 BARS

The chord progression starts on Amin7 the IImin7 chord in the key of G maj followed by the D7 chord the V chord in the key of Gmaj. The progression outlined is a II V I in Gmaj followed by the IV chord Cmaj7#11.

The next 4 bars outline the II V I in Minor. eg F# half diminished - B7b9 - Emin7 .

E min7 is the relative minor of G major.

Notice that the chords are all derived from the G major scale except the B7b9 in bar 6 and the E7 in the 8th bar. These chords are funtioning as V chords. The B7b9 is the V chord of the Emin7.

The E7 is the V of II min7 chord Amin7.

Notice in the 6th bar on the B7b9 chord the bass line descends from B down the G major scale, whats being outlined is the B7b9 b13 scale.

By referring to the chord chart on the previous page notice the difference between the chords on bars 8 and 16. Bar 8 is Emin7 - E7 eg the E7 takes us back to the Amin7.

In the 16th bar Emin7 is the final chord. This is because the tune resolves in E minor before going to the second half of the tune.

©Waterfall Publishing House 2012

Jazz standard chord progression # 1 in 12 keys

APPLYING THE II V I IN MAJOR MODULATING TO II V I INTO THE RELATIVE MINOR

©Waterfall Publishing House 2012

©Waterfall Publishing House 2012

G#ø C#7(b9) F#MIN7

G#ø C#7(b9) F#MIN7

BMIN7 E7 AMAJ7 DMAJ7#11

G#ø C#7(b9) F#MIN7 F7#11 EMIN7 Eb7#11

DMAJ7#11 G#ø C#7(b9) F#MIN7

Bb Major

CMIN7 F7 BbMAJ EbMAJ7#11

Aø D7(b9) GMIN7 G7

CMIN7 F7 BbMAJ EbMAJ7#11

Aø D7(b9) GMIN7

Aø D7(b9) GMIN7 G7

©Waterfall Publishing House 2012

©Waterfall Publishing House 2012

Emaj7#11 B♭ø E♭7(♭9) A♭min7

C Major

Dmin7 G7 Cmaj7 Fmaj7#11

Bø E7(♭9) Amin7 A7

Dmin7 G7 Cmaj7 Fmaj7#11

Bø E7(♭9) Amin7

Bø E7(♭9) Amin7 A7

Dmin7 G7 Cmaj7 Fmaj7#11

Bø E7(♭9) Amin7 A♭7#11 Gmin7 G♭7#11

Fmaj7#11 Bø E7(♭9) Amin7

Db Major

©Waterfall Publishing House 2012

©Waterfall Publishing House 2012

©Waterfall Publishing House 2012

©Waterfall Publishing House 2012

©Waterfall Publishing House 2012

F⌀ B♭7(♭9) E♭MIN7 E♭7

A♭MIN7 D♭7 G♭MAJ7 BMAJ7#11

F⌀ B♭7(♭9) E♭MIN7

F⌀ B♭7(♭9) E♭MIN7 E♭7

A♭MIN7 D♭7 G♭MAJ7 BMAJ7#11

F⌀ B♭7(♭9) E♭MIN7 D7#11 D♭MIN7 C#7#11

BMAJ7#11 F⌀ B♭7(♭9) E♭MIN7

Chapter 3

THE I VI II V PROGRESSION IN 12 KEYS

The I VI II V progression, like the II V I progression is one of the most commonly used chord progressions in the jazz standard vocabulary. The I VI II V progression is leading to the root by modulating through the cycle of 4ths.
Many of the " altered " turnarounds are derived from the I VI II V progression.

Ex.1 shows the diatonic 7ths chart in the key of Bb major and outlines the relationships of the chords in t he I VI II V progression

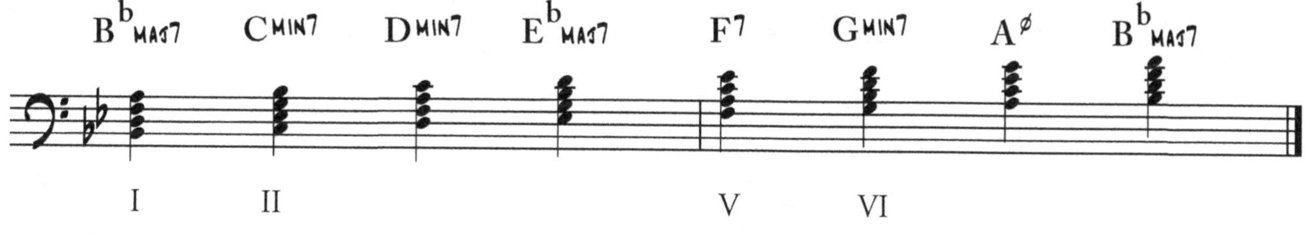

©Waterfall Publishing House 2012

Ex. 2 shows the I VI II V I progression in Bb major outlining the relationship of the cycle of fourths. Notice that the cycle of 4ths starts at the Gmin7 chord and modulates around the cycle. Gmin7 Cmin7 F7 until the progression resolves to the tonic eg. Bb major7

BbMAJ7
GMIN7
CMIN7
F7
BbMAJ7
I
VI
II
V
I
cycle of 4ths
up 4th
up 4th
up 4th
resolves to tonic

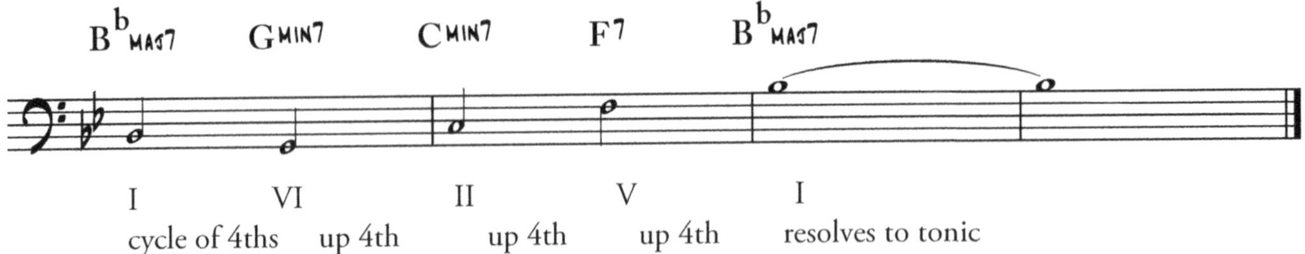

THE I VI II V OVER 2 BARS

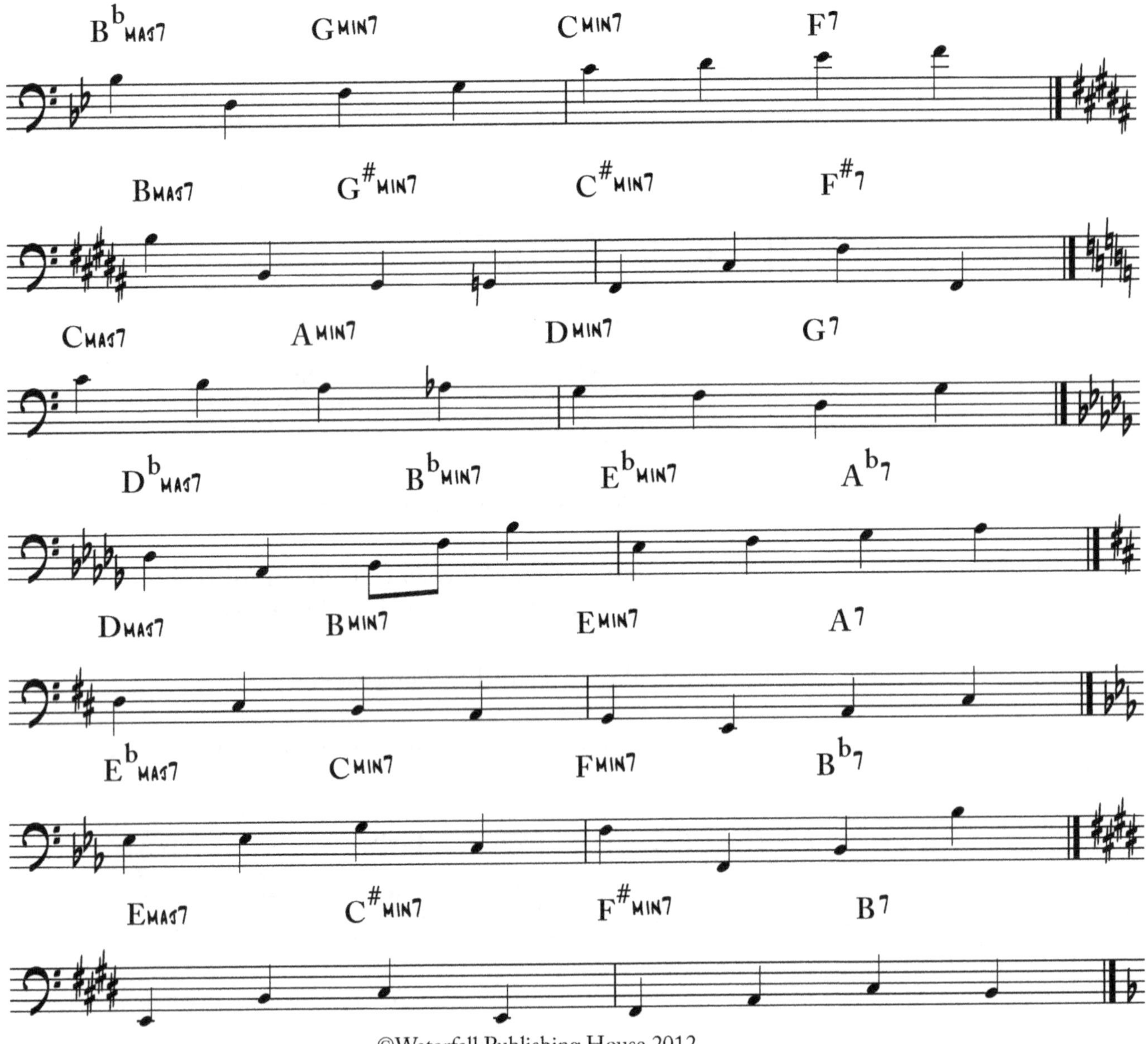

BbMAJ7
GMIN7
CMIN7
F7
BMAJ7
G#MIN7
C#MIN7
F#7
CMAJ7
AMIN7
DMIN7
G7
DbMAJ7
BbMIN7
EbMIN7
Ab7
DMAJ7
BMIN7
EMIN7
A7
EbMAJ7
CMIN7
FMIN7
Bb7
EMAJ7
C#MIN7
F#MIN7
B7

©Waterfall Publishing House 2012

THE I VI II V PROGRESSION OVER 4 BARS

©Waterfall Publishing House 2012

©Waterfall Publishing House 2012

Chapter 4 The I VI II V PROGRESSION AND THE SECONDARY DOMINANT CHORD

** SECONDARY DOMINANT CHORDS **

The term Secondary Dominant is a term used regularly in jazz theory and harmony.

The following example shows the Diatonic 7th chords in the key of Ab major.
By refering to the diatonic 7ths chord chart we know that the II III & VI chords are min7 chords.
In the key of Abmaj the II chord is Bbmin7, the III chord is Cmin7, & the VI chord is Fmin7.
The minor 7th chords can also be made dominant, this is known as a Secondary Dominant chord.

In the key of Ab major the secondary dominant chords are Bb7, C7 and F7.

Example 2 shows the secondary dominant chords related to the key of Ab major.

By refering to the original example of the diatonic 7th chords in the key of Ab notice that the IImin7 chord Bbmin7 is now II7 Bb7.
The IIImin7 chord Cmin7 is now II7 C7.
The VImin7 chord Fmin7 is now VI7 F7.

©Waterfall Publishing House 2012

THE V of V CYCLE

A common chord sequence which is often associated with secondary dominant chords is the V of V cycle.
The V of V cycle moves around the circle of 4ths. eg. up a 4th or down a 5th.

The next example shows the I VI II V progression in Ab major incorporating secondary dominant chords and the V of V cycle.

Ex. 3 Notice now the VI chord the Fmin7 is now F7, this is functioning as a secondary dominant chord eg V of V F7 is the V chord leading to Bb.

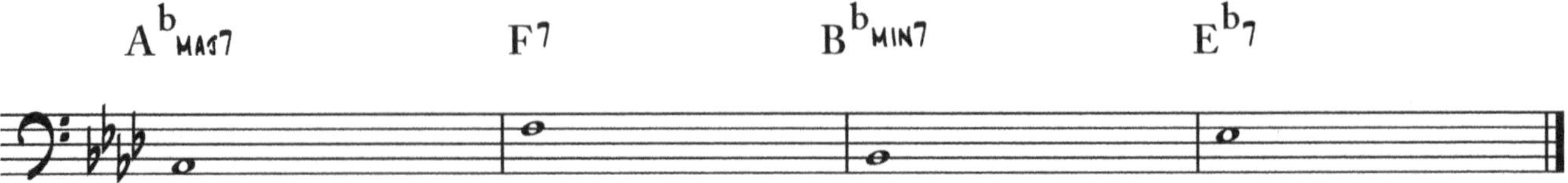

Ex. 4 Shows the first 8 measures of Jazz standard chord progression #2 notice now the IImin7 chord Bbmin7 is now Bb7 once again functioning as a secondary dominant chord eg V of V Bb7 is the V chord leading to Eb. The complete progression is I VI II V III VI II V.

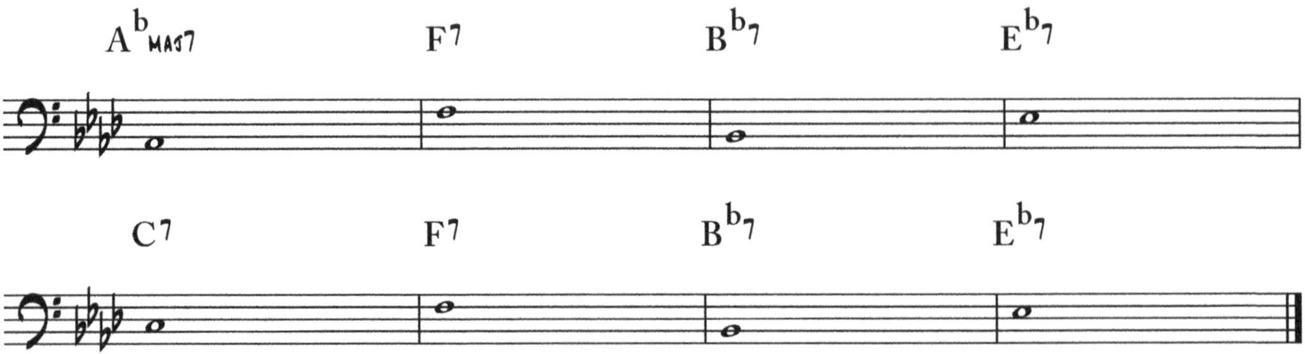

Jazz standard #2 outlines the use of the secondary dominant chords shown above and bass lines are written out in all 12 keys.
This is a classic standard played in all 12 keys by the be bop musicians.

©Waterfall Publishing House 2012

Jazz standard chord progression # 2 in 12 keys

APPLYING THE USE OF SECONDARY DOMINANT CHORDS

©Waterfall Publishing House 2012

©Waterfall Publishing House 2012

©Waterfall Publishing House 2012

C Major

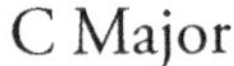

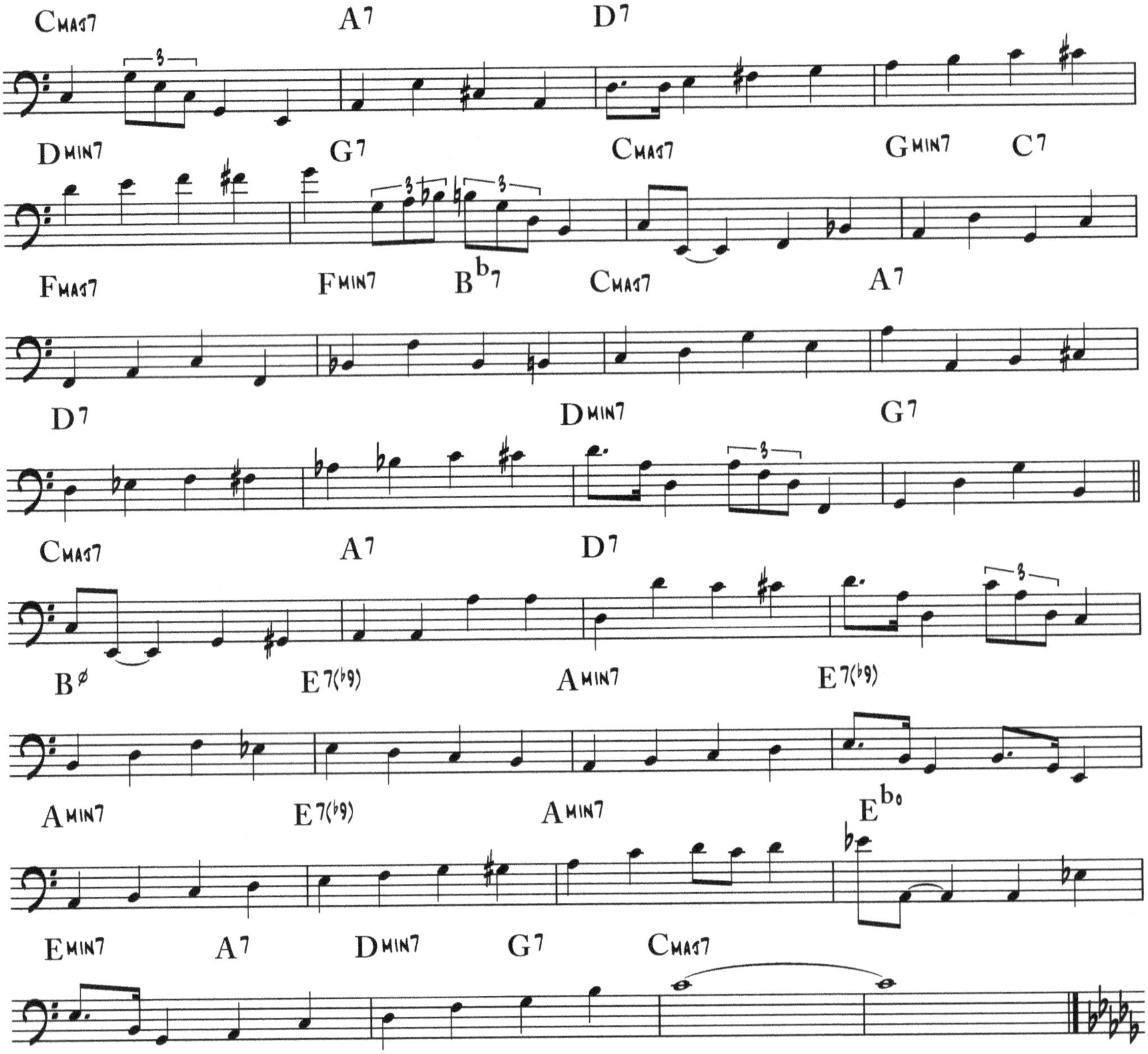
CMAJ7
A7
D7
DMIN7
G7
CMAJ7
GMIN7
C7
FMAJ7
FMIN7
Bb7
CMAJ7
A7
D7
DMIN7
G7
CMAJ7
A7
D7
Bø
E7(b9)
AMIN7
E7(b9)
AMIN7
E7(b9)
AMIN7
Ebo
EMIN7
A7
DMIN7
G7
CMAJ7

Db Major

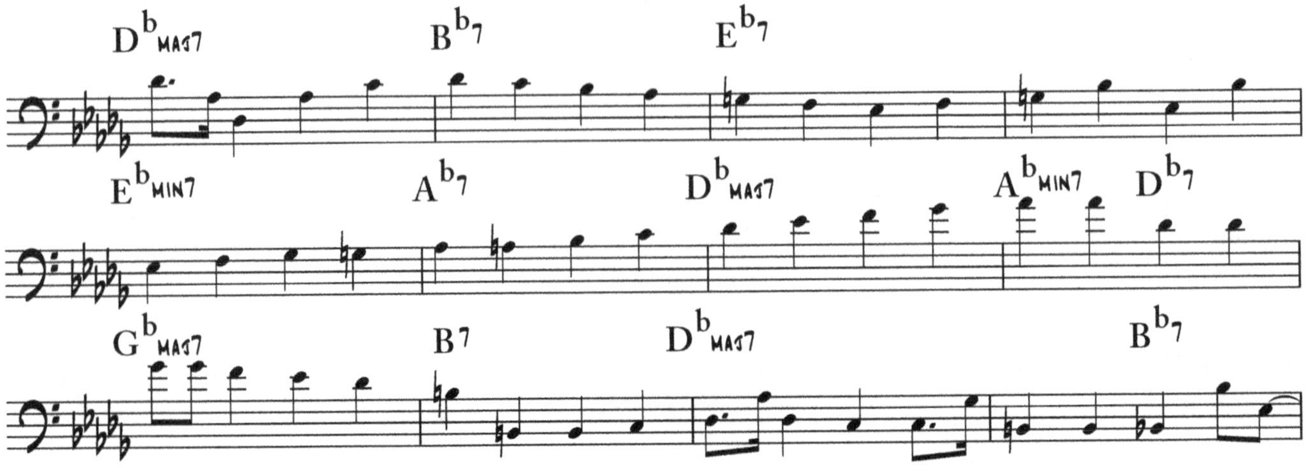
DbMAJ7
Bb7
Eb7
EbMIN7
Ab7
DbMAJ7
AbMIN7
Db7
GbMAJ7
B7
DbMAJ7
Bb7

©Waterfall Publishing House 2012

©Waterfall Publishing House 2012

©Waterfall Publishing House 2012

©Waterfall Publishing House 2012

©Waterfall Publishing House 2012

©Waterfall Publishing House 2012

Chapter 5 THE I IV III VI PROGRESSION IN 12 KEYS.

The I IV III VI chord progression is often used as the turnaround into the II chord.
By refering again to the diatonic 7ths in the key of Bb major shown below, the I IV III VI relationship is outlined.
In the example shown below notice that the VI chord is dominant. eg G7, this is an example of the VI chord functioning as a secondary dominant chord. In this example the V of II. eg G will be modulating to C.

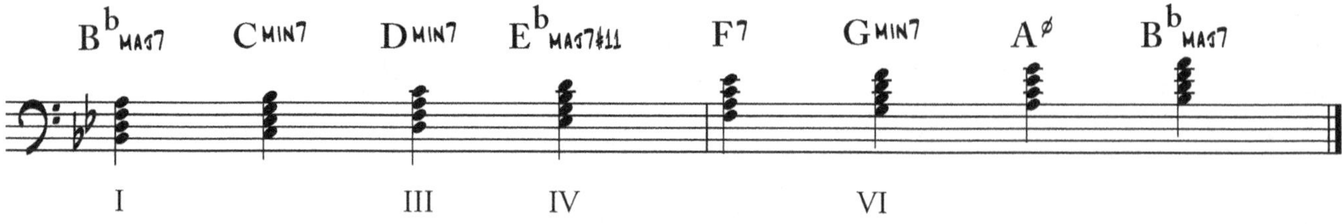

Ex. 2 Notice in this example the I IV III VI progression continues on into the II V I in Bb. The cycle is resolved. eg I IV III VI II V I.

THE I IV III VI II V PROGRESSION IN 12 KEYS.

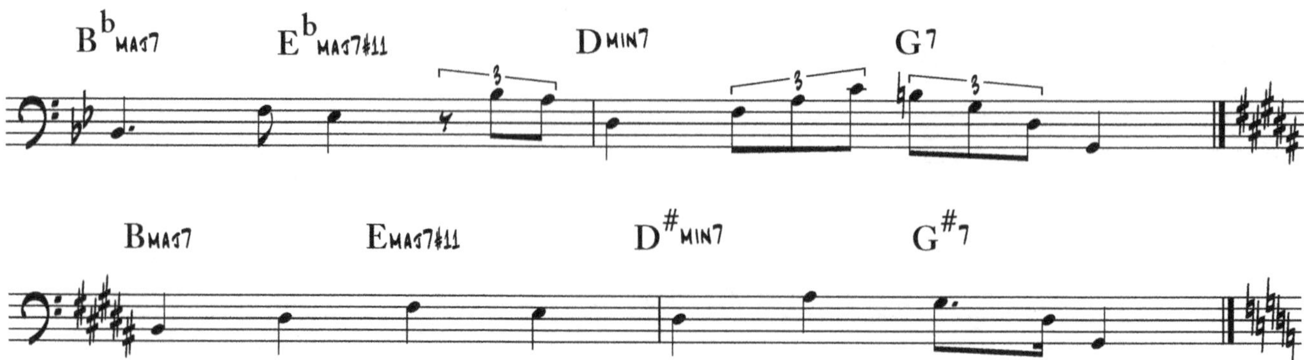

©Waterfall Publishing House 2012

©Waterfall Publishing House 2012

Chapter 6 THE bVII DOMINANT 7 TH CHORD & THE IV MINOR bVII 7 PROGRESSION

In the following chapter we will look at the b7 VII chord and its function in standard chord progressions. The b7 VII chord is functioning like a V7 chord, it wants to resolve, it is bringing you back to the tonic or root. The progression is often preceeded by the relative II min7 in this case it is known as the IV min7. In some progressions the IV min7 chord will lead to the root or tonic without using the b7 VII chord. This occurs frequently in the turnaround into bridges and endings of tunes.
The move of IV min7 to b7 VII is sometimes called a minor third substitute.
The following examples outline this example in more detail.

Ex. 1 Below we have the progression Dmin7 - G7 Cmaj7 or II V I.

Now we look at the progression Fmin7 -Bb7 - Cmaj7 or IVmin7- b7 VII - I.
By looking at the example of the diatonic 7ths in Eb we can see where the Fmin7 and Bb7 are coming from, and why it is sometimes referred to as a minor third substitute. The II V progession Fmin7 Bb7 comes from the key of Eb major. Eb as we know is a minor third or 3 half steps away from the key of C. With the progression Fmin7 Bb7 Cmaj7 we are in the key of Eb major a minor third above the tonic key of C major for 2 measures then resolve to C major via the Bb7 the bVII 7 chord in the key of C.

Ex. 2

Ex. 3 Diatonic 7ths in the key of Ebmajor

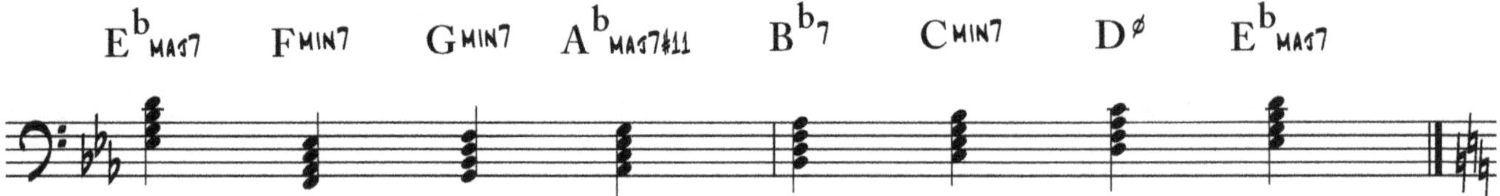

To summarize we can look at the chart of the diatonic 7ths in the key of C the IV chord is maj7#11 and the VII chord is half diminished.
However we substitute Fmin7 eg IV min7 and Bb7 b7 VII. Note that the Bb is a whole step down from C, this is where the term b7 VII chord comes from.
As you learn tunes you will see this progression come up time and time again, and when you have mastered the concept for yourself you will be able to substitute the progression on the fly. Before substituting chords check them against the melody to see if the substituted chords fit with the melody line.

Ex. 4

©Waterfall Publishing House 2012

THE IV MIN7 bVII 7 PROGRESSION IN 12 KEYS

©Waterfall Publishing House 2012

Chapter 7 THE IV MAJOR TO IV MINOR bVII 7 PROGRESSION IN 12 KEYS

The following progression is another one of the standard chord sequences used in the standard jazz vocabulary. The move outlines the modulation of IV major to I major through the IVmin7 bVII7 progression. The progression is IV major7#11 / IVmin7 bVII7 / I maj7.

The example below outlines the progression in detail in the key of Bb major.

IV major7#11 / IVmin7 bVII7 / I maj7 in 12 keys

©Waterfall Publishing House 2012

©Waterfall Publishing House 2012

Chapter 8

THE TURNAROUND INTO THE II CHORD & THE APPLICATION OF THE I IV III VI PROGRESSION.

Jazz standard #3 is a classic standard chord progression that contains all of the harmonic material covered in the book so far.
The tune outlines the II V progression, I VI7 II V , IV major to IV minor , and the bVII to I followed by the I IV III VI progression often used as the turnaround into the II chord.
Notice the 1st chord in measure # 1 of the tune is C7. The tune starts on the II chord, usually the II chord is minor eg part of a II V I progression.
In this tune the starting chord is the II7 chord, this chord is functioning as a secondary dominant chord as part of a V of V cycle.

As we know the minor chords in the major key can be made secondary dominant chords.
By refering to the diatonic 7ths chord chart in the key of Bb major , the minor chords are outlined eg II III VI.
Cmin 7 , Dmin7, Gmin7 are the minor chords in the key of Bb, and these chords can be used as secondary dominant chords eg C7 D7 G7.

Ex. 1 Shows the diatonic chord chart in the key of Bb major.

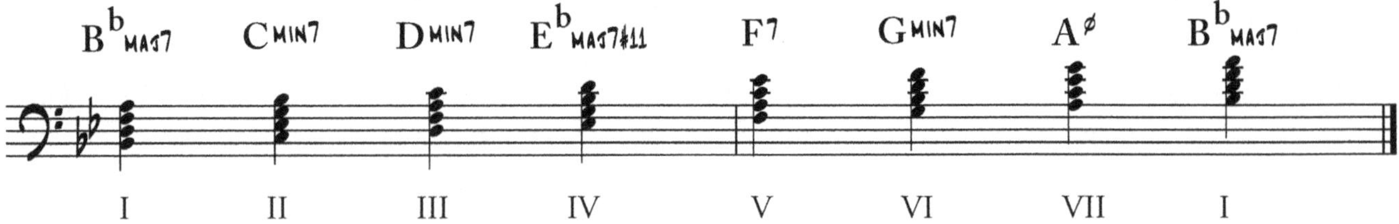

Ex. 2 shows the first 8 measures of the tune, outlining the II7 chord and the V of V cycle.
C7 to F7 is a modulation down a 5th eg V of V. The Cmin7 or IImin7 is the relative IImin7 of the F7 eg II V I in Bbmajor.

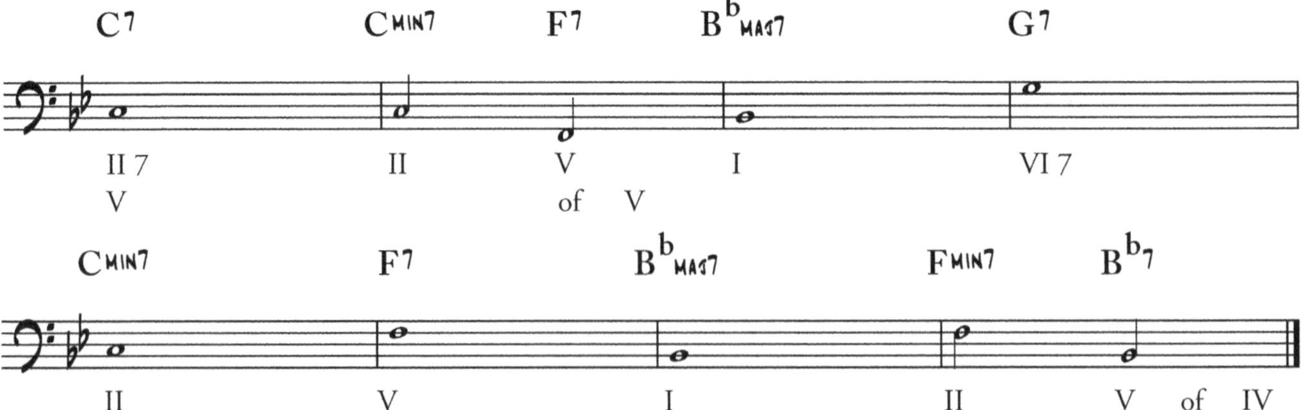

©Waterfall Publishing House 2012

Ex. 3 shows the last 8 measures of the tune with the I IV III VI progression used in the last 2 measures as the turnaround into the II7 chord C7.

Eb MAJ7#11 Eb MIN7 Ab 7#11 Bb MAJ7 G7
IV maj IV min7 bVII7 I VI
C MIN7 F7 Bb MAJ7 Eb MAJ7#11 D MIN7 G7
II V I IV III VI

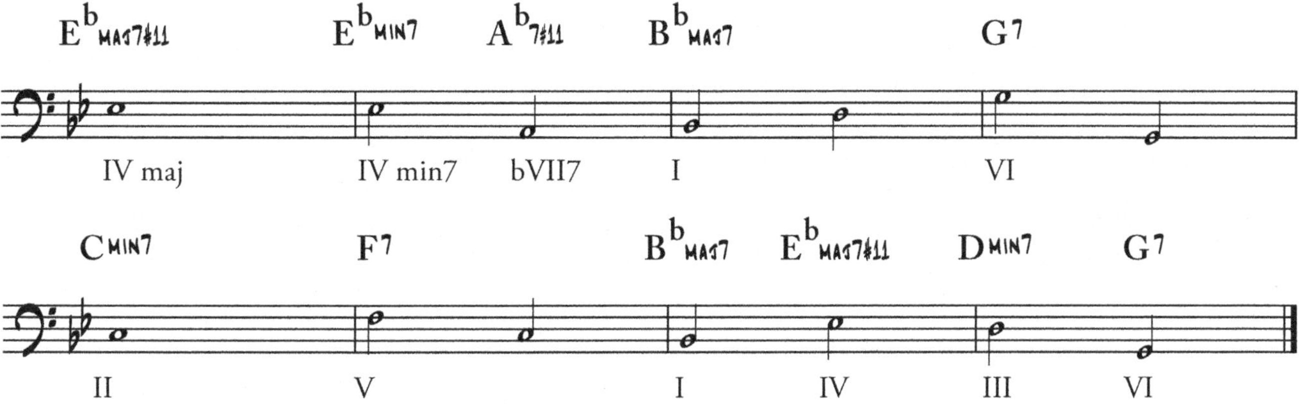

Ex. 4 shows the complete digital analysis of jazz standard # 3.
Notice the difference in the turnarounds in the 1st and 2nd endings in measures 15 - 16 & measures 31 - 32 . This is because in the last 2 measures of the tune measures 31 - 32 the chord structure resolves to the tonic key Bb major before returning to the top of the tune.

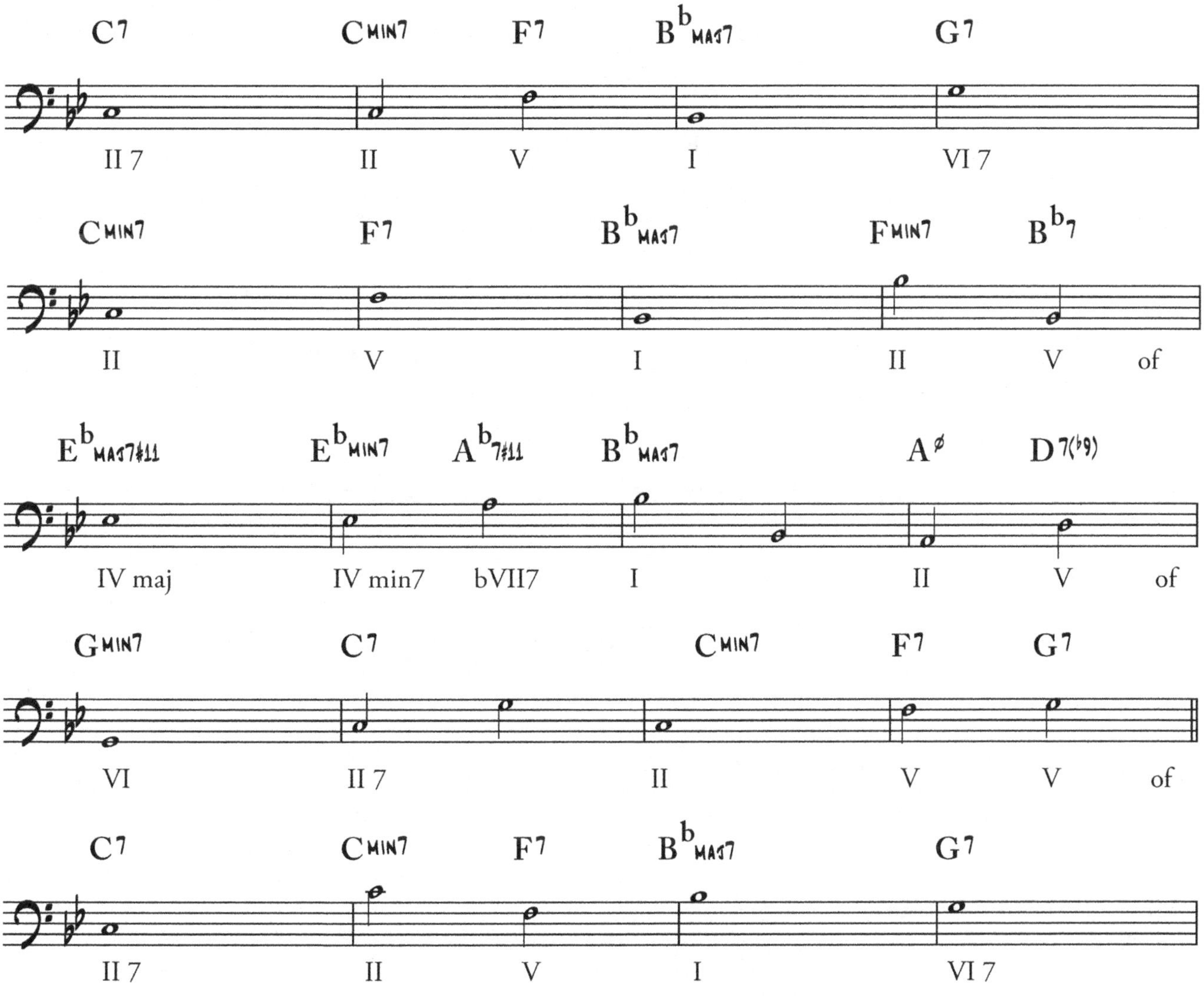
C7 C MIN7 F7 Bb MAJ7 G7
II 7 II V I VI 7
C MIN7 F7 Bb MAJ7 F MIN7 Bb7
II V I II V of
Eb MAJ7#11 Eb MIN7 Ab 7#11 Bb MAJ7 A Ø D 7(b9)
IV maj IV min7 bVII7 I II V of
G MIN7 C7 C MIN7 F7 G7
VI II 7 II V V of
C7 C MIN7 F7 Bb MAJ7 G7
II 7 II V I VI 7

©Waterfall Publishing House 2012

CMIN7 F7 BbMAJ7 FMIN7 Bb7
II V I II V of
EbMAJ7#11 EbMIN7 Ab7#11 BbMAJ7 G7
IV maj IV min7 bVII7 I II V of
CMIN7 F7 BbMAJ7 EbMAJ7#11 DMIN7 G7
II V I IV III VI

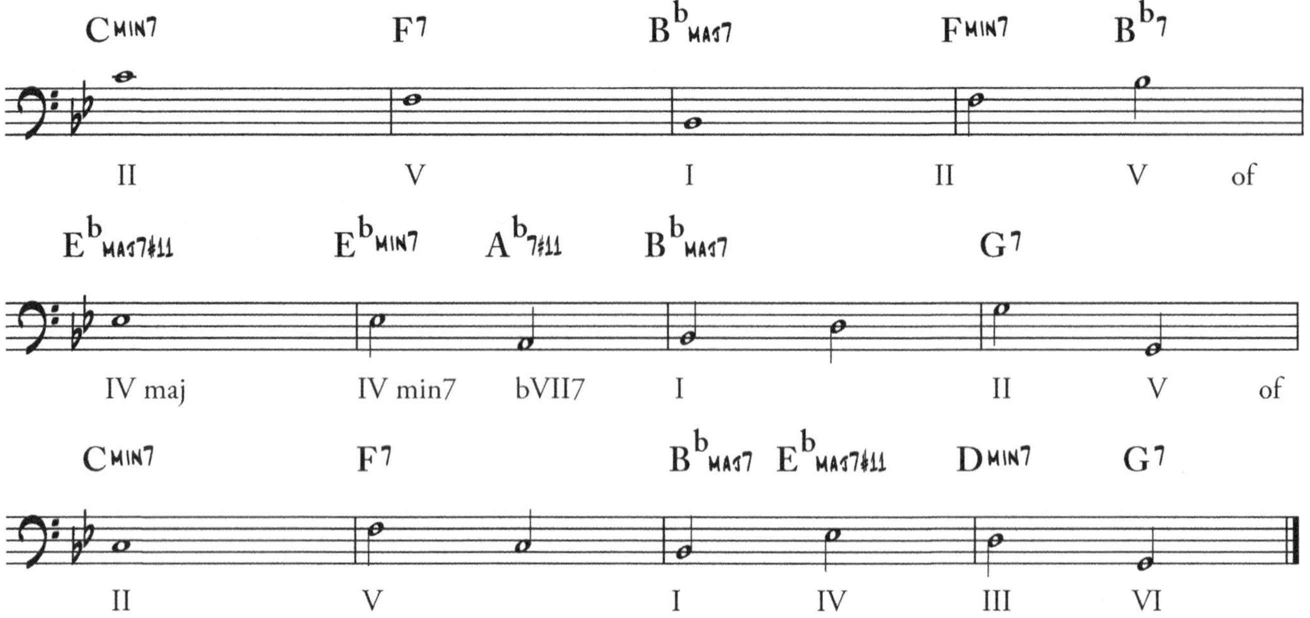

Jazz standard chord progression # 3 in 12 keys

TURNAROUND INTO THE II CHORD & THE APPLICATION OF THE I IV III VI PROGRESSION

Bb Major

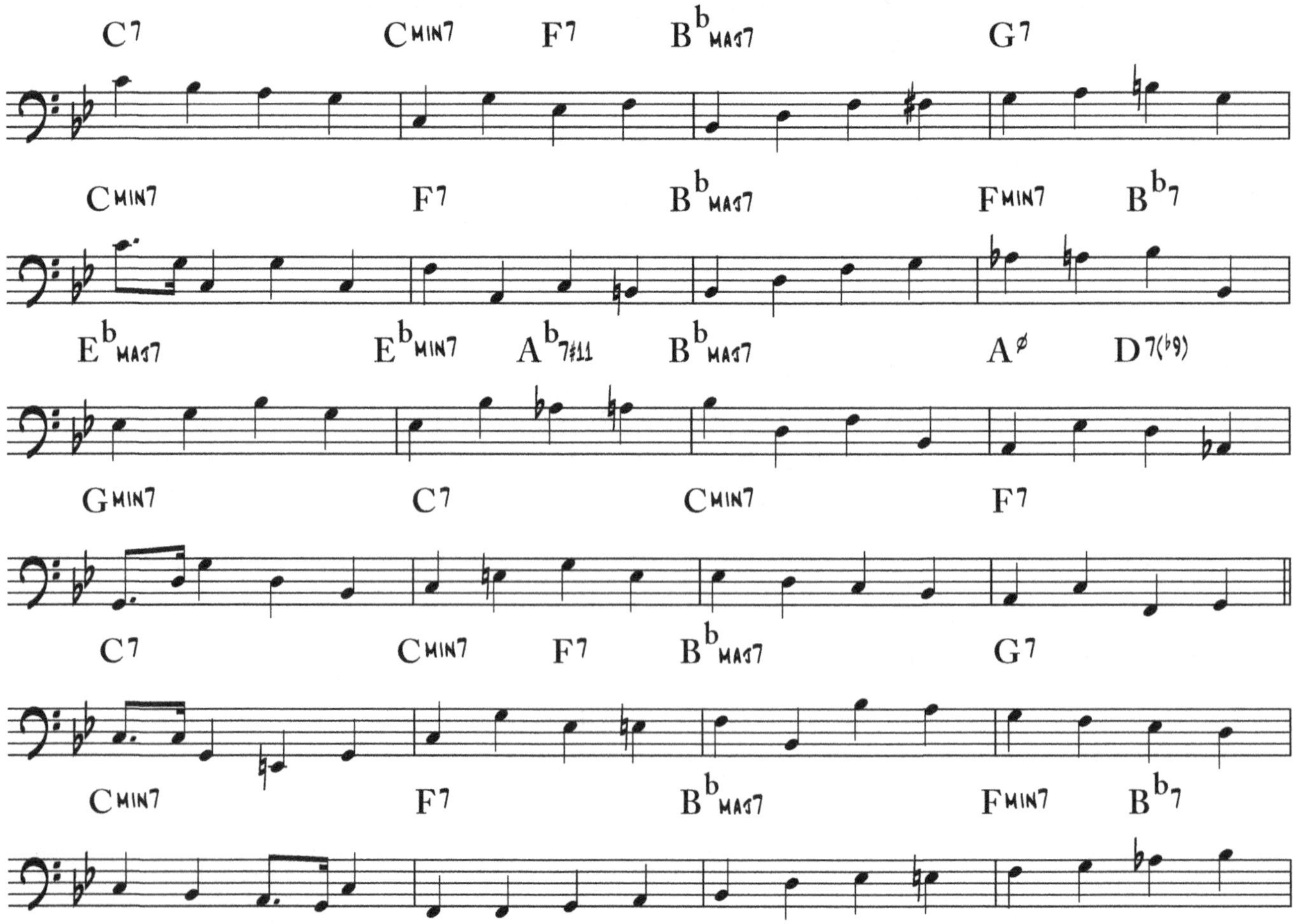
C7 CMIN7 F7 BbMAJ7 G7
CMIN7 F7 BbMAJ7 FMIN7 Bb7
EbMAJ7 EbMIN7 Ab7#11 BbMAJ7 Aø D7(b9)
GMIN7 C7 CMIN7 F7
C7 CMIN7 F7 BbMAJ7 G7
CMIN7 F7 BbMAJ7 FMIN7 Bb7

©Waterfall Publishing House 2012

©Waterfall Publishing House 2012

C Major

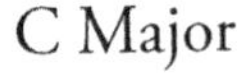

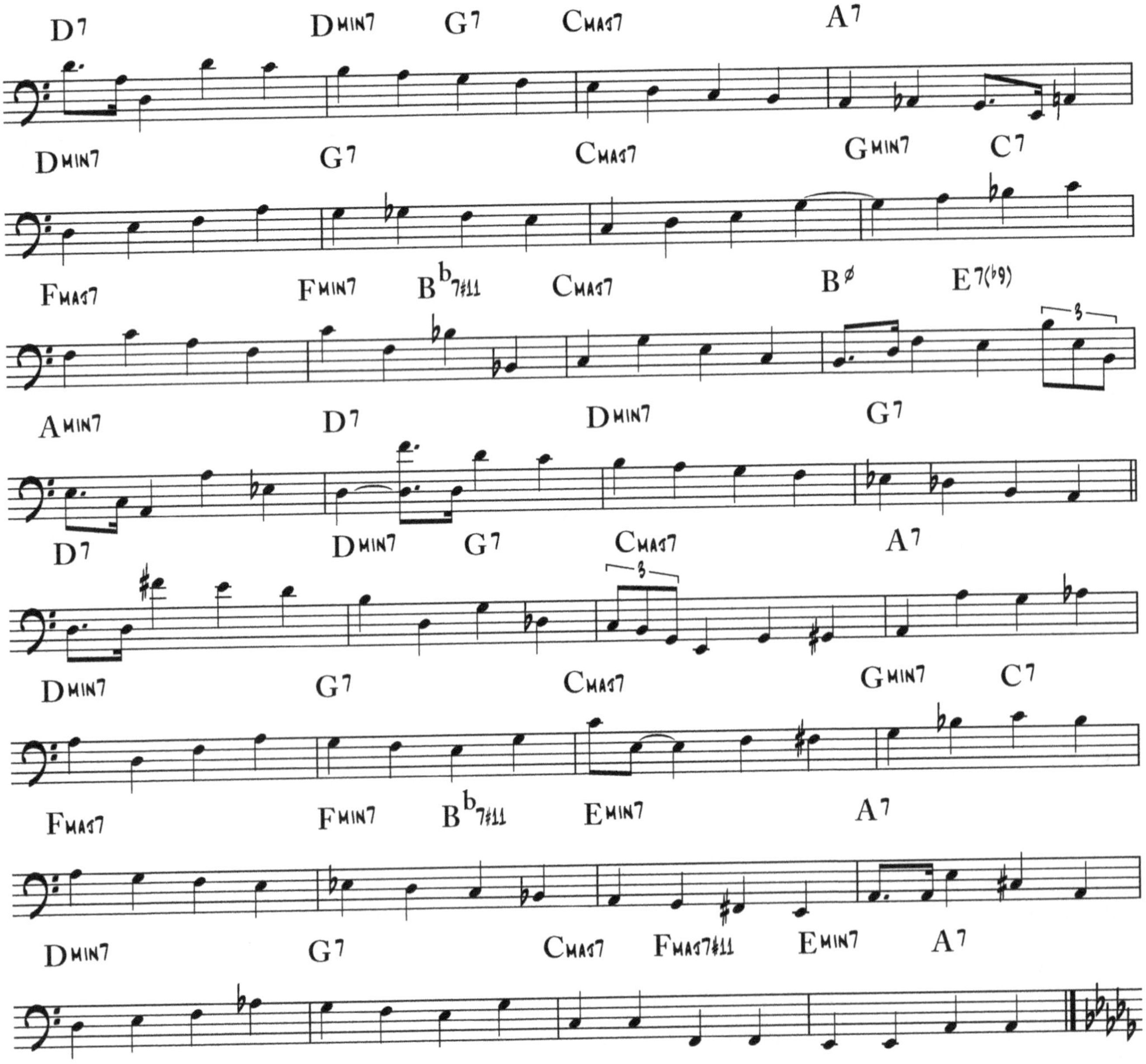
D7 Dmin7 G7 Cmaj7 A7
Dmin7 G7 Cmaj7 Gmin7 C7
Fmaj7 Fmin7 Bb7#11 Cmaj7 Bø E7(b9)
Amin7 D7 Dmin7 G7
D7 Dmin7 G7 Cmaj7 A7
Dmin7 G7 Cmaj7 Gmin7 C7
Fmaj7 Fmin7 Bb7#11 Emin7 A7
Dmin7 G7 Cmaj7 Fmaj7#11 Emin7 A7

Db Major

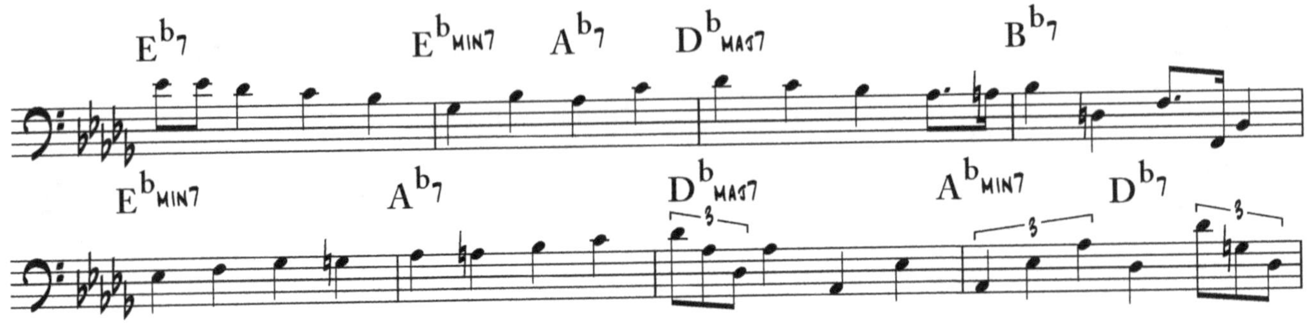
Eb7 Ebmin7 Ab7 Dbmaj7 Bb7
Ebmin7 Ab7 Dbmaj7 Abmin7 Db7

©Waterfall Publishing House 2012

©Waterfall Publishing House 2012

©Waterfall Publishing House 2012

E Major

F#7 F#MIN7 B7 EMAJ7 C#7

F#MIN7 B7 EMAJ7 BMIN7 E7

AMAJ7 AMIN7 D7#11 EMAJ7 D#ø G#7(b9)

C#MIN7 F#7 F#MIN7 B7

F#7 F#MIN7 B7 EMAJ7 C#7

F#MIN7 B7 EMAJ7 BMIN7 E7

AMAJ7 AMIN7 D7#11 EMAJ7 C#7

F#MIN7 B7 EMAJ7 AMAJ7#11 G#MIN7 C#7

F Major

G7 GMIN7 C7 FMAJ7 D7

GMIN7 C7 FMAJ7 CMIN7 F7

©Waterfall Publishing House 2012

©Waterfall Publishing House 2012

©Waterfall Publishing House 2012

©Waterfall Publishing House 2012

Having covered the material in the book so far and having played through the previous tune in all 12 keys the bassist can begin to understand and see the advantages of being able to recognise and identify chord progressions.

By practicing these common chord sequences in 12 keys, the task of learing tunes in 12 keys becomes more managable.

It still takes work, however instead of thinking of 32 bars or 36 bars etc were thinking of the relationship of the harmonic modulations in the tune.

By practicing the material in this book in twelve keys you will have a vast amount of the jazz standard vocabulary under your fingers in all 12 keys. This makes it easier to come to terms with changing keys on the bandstand.

©Waterfall Publishing House 2012

Chapter 9

TURNAROUND INTO THE IV CHORD IN 12 KEYS

In previous chapters we looked at the IV major to IVminor modulation, another common harmonic device in the jazz standard vocabulary is to start the tune on the IV major chord. In this chapter we outline the turnaround into the IV chord.

The following standard chord progression starts on the IV major chord and modulates to the tonic Key via the IV min7 b7 VII chord. This is another common chord sequence in the jazz standard vocabulary. This progresion is followed by the turnaround into the IV major chord in 12 keys.

Ex. 1 shows the Diatonic 7ths chart in the key of Bb major.

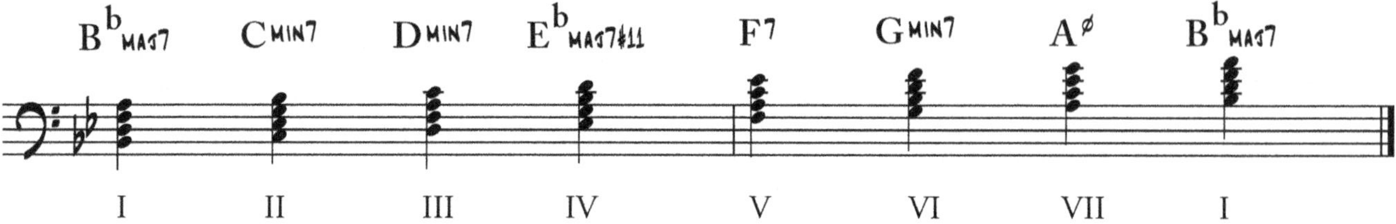

Ex. 2 shows the first 8 measures of jazz standard #4. The tune starts on Ebmaj #11 , by reviewing the diatonic chart in the key of Bb major we know that the Ebmaj7 is the IV chord in the key of Bb major. The chord then modulates to the tonickey Bbmajor via the IV min7 b VII7 progression *.

* The IV min7 bVII 7 chord progression can also be thought of as minor third substitute.
In the example shown in jazz standard # 4 the chord progression Ebmin7 Ab7 leads to Bb major 7 this is a deceptive cadence.
Ebmin7 Ab7 is a II V from the key of Dbmajor. The II V progression leading to Bbmajor7 is Cmin7 F7.
Bb maj and Db major are a minor third apart. eg the term minor third substitute.
This topic has been covered in greater detail in Constructing Walking Jazz Bass Lines Book III - Standard Lines.

When learning a new tune or seeing a tune on the bandstand for the first time, try to analyse the tune before its counted off.
When dealing with a tune that starts on a IV major chord, as a general rule of thumb if you see the tune start on a major 7 #11 chord its a pretty safe bet its the IV chord. Then look at the turnaround in the last few measures of the tune to see where the tune resolves. This relates to functional harmony.
This method may not work in non functional or contemporary chord progressions.

©Waterfall Publishing House 2012

Ex. 3 shows the first 16 measures of jazz standard # 4, Notice in the last 2 measures bars 15 - 16 the turnaround into the second half of the tune eg. the IV chord Ebmaj7.

The turnaround consists of the V of V cylce with the relative IImin7 chords. eg Cmin7 F7 Fmin7 Bb7

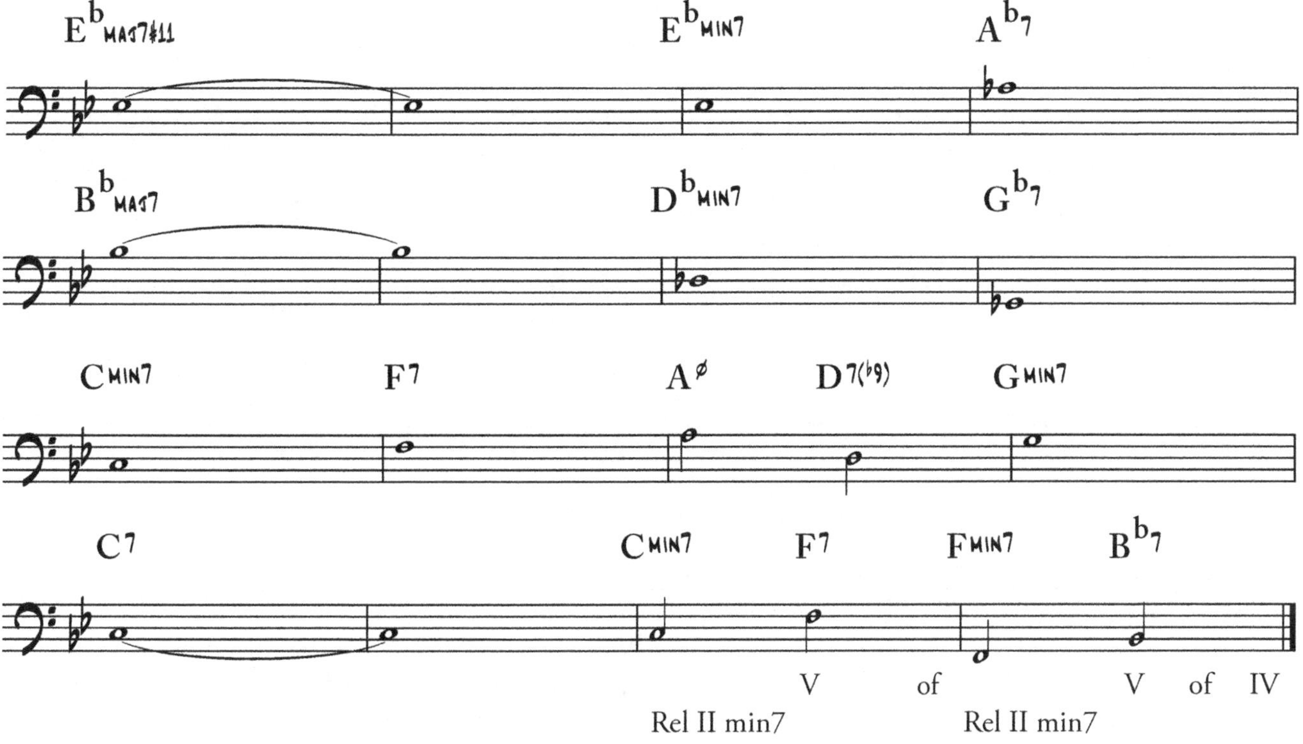

Ex. 4 shows the second 16 measures of jazz standard # 4, Notice in the last 2 measures bars 31 - 32 the turnaround into the top of the tune eg. the IV chord Ebmaj7.

The turnaround resolves to the tonic key or I chord Bb major and then modulates to the Ebmaj7 chord via the Fmin7 Bb7 progression.

©Waterfall Publishing House 2012

Jazz standard chord progression # 4 in 12 keys

THE APPLICATION OF THE TURNAROUND INTO THE IV CHORD IN 12 KEYS

©Waterfall Publishing House 2012

©Waterfall Publishing House 2012

CMAJ7 EbMIN7 Ab7

DMIN7 G7 Bø E7(b9) AMIN7

D7 DMIN7 G7 CMAJ7 GMIN7 C7

Db Major

GbMAJ7#11 GbMIN7 Cb7

DbMAJ7 EMIN7 A7

EbMIN7 Ab7 Cø F7(b9) BbMIN7

Eb7 EbMIN7 Ab7 AbMIN7 Db7

GbMAJ#11 GbMIN7 Cb7

DbMAJ7 EMIN7 A7

EbMIN7 Ab7 Cø F7(b9) BbMIN7

Eb7 EbMIN7 Ab7 DbMAJ7 AbMIN7 Db7

©Waterfall Publishing House 2012

D Major

©Waterfall Publishing House 2012

©Waterfall Publishing House 2012

©Waterfall Publishing House 2012

F# Major

©Waterfall Publishing House 2012

©Waterfall Publishing House 2012

AbMAJ7
BMIN7
E7
BbMIN7
Eb7
Gø
C7(b9)
FMIN7
Bb7
BbMIN7
Eb7
AbMAJ7
EbMIN7
Ab7

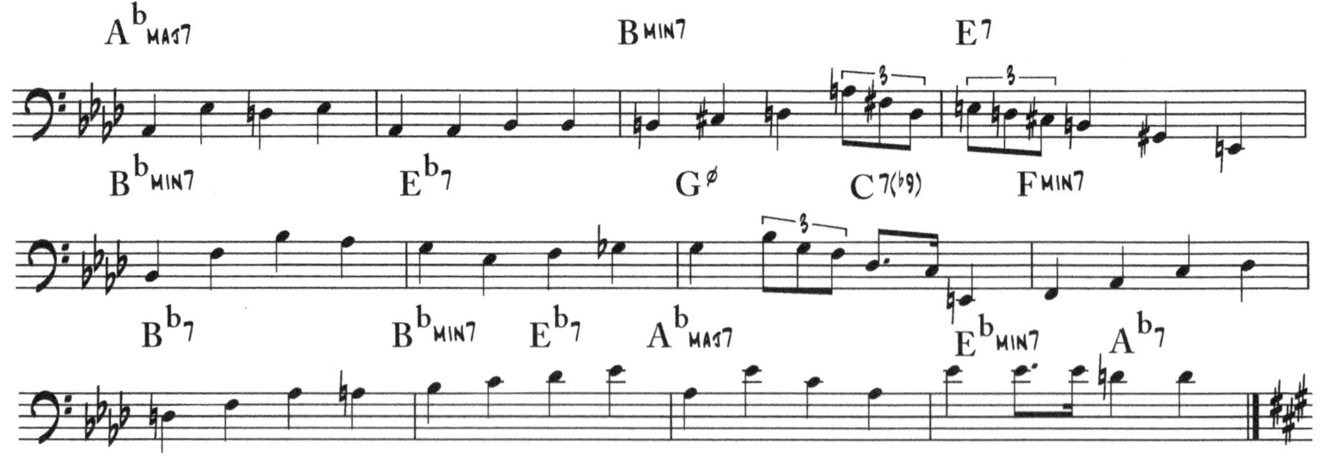

A Major

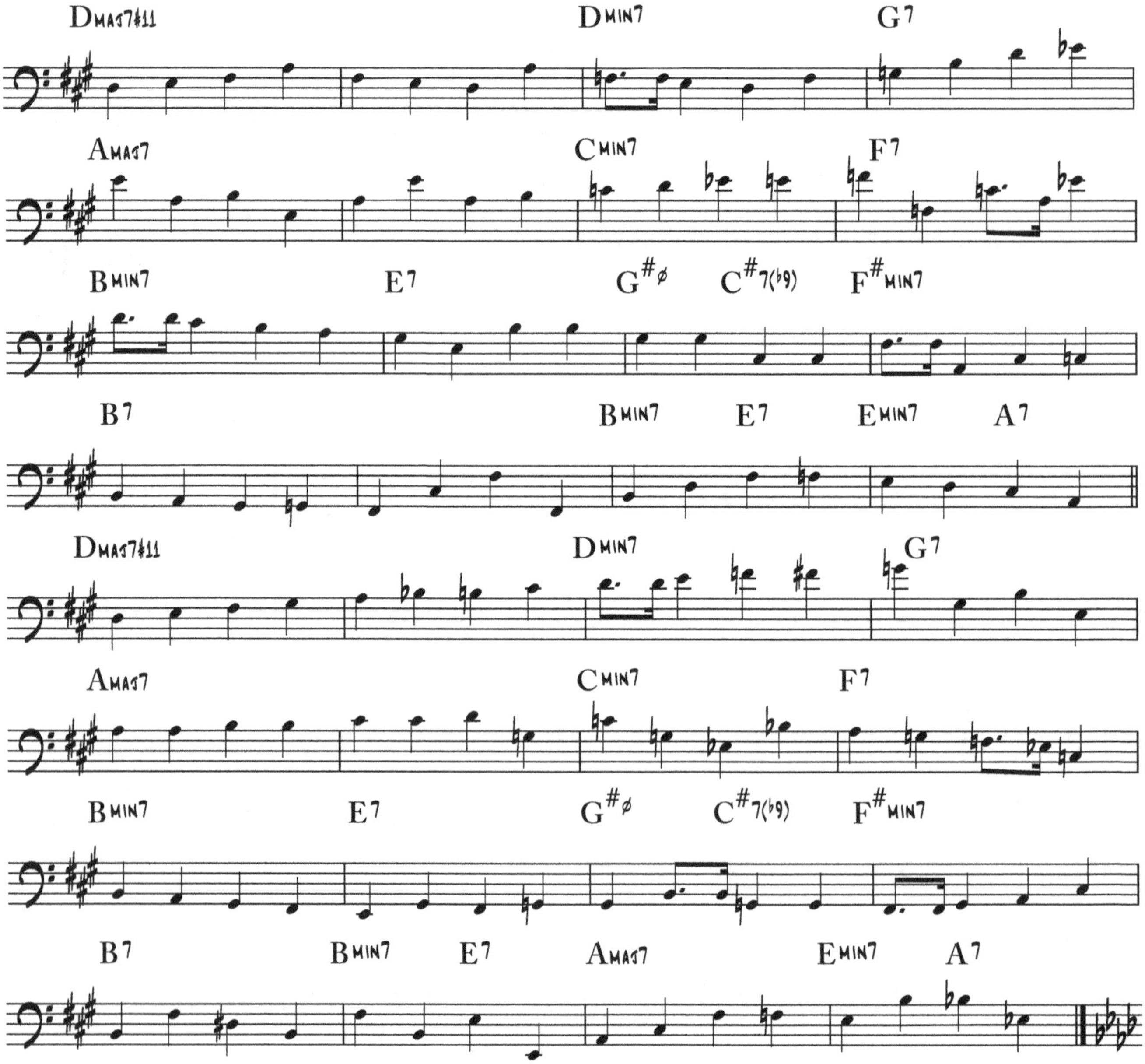
DMAJ7#11
DMIN7
G7
AMAJ7
CMIN7
F7
BMIN7
E7
G#ø
C#7(b9)
F#MIN7
B7
BMIN7
E7
EMIN7
A7
DMAJ7#11
DMIN7
G7
AMAJ7
CMIN7
F7
BMIN7
E7
G#ø
C#7(b9)
F#MIN7
B7
BMIN7
E7
AMAJ7
EMIN7
A7

©Waterfall Publishing House 2012

Chapter 10 THE TURNAROUND INTO THE VI MINOR CHORD

The following standard chord progression starts on the VI min7 chord and modulates to the I chord Abmaj. This is another classic jazz standard played and practiced in all 12 keys. The form is A B C D and is 36 measures long.

The first example shows the A section, the first 8 measures of the tune. By refering again to the diatonic 7ths chart, the relationship of the VI min chord is outlined.

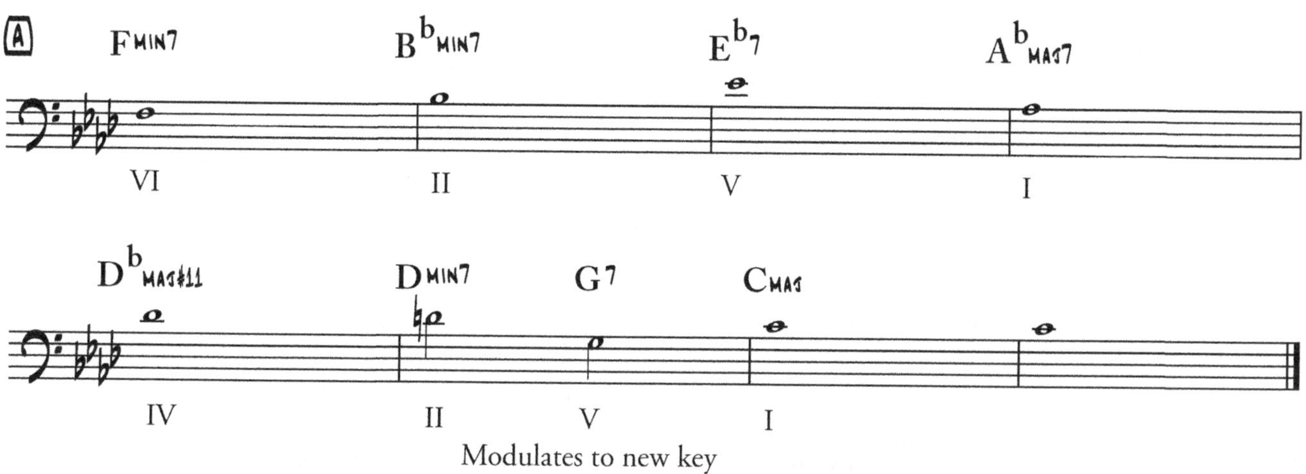

Ex. 2 Diatonic 7ths in the key of Ab major

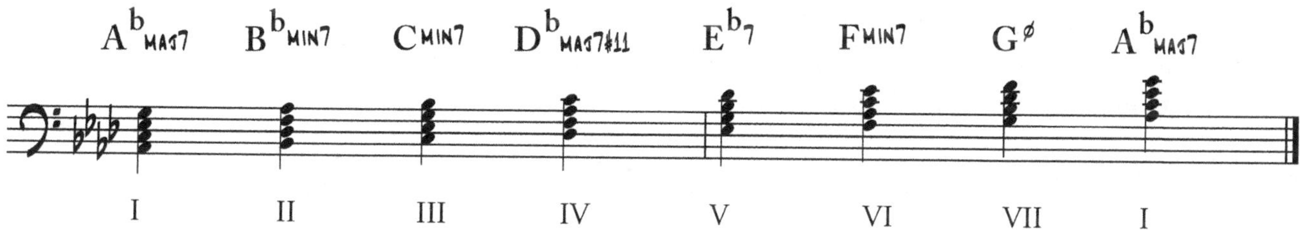

Ex. 3 Shows the B section, the second 8 measures of the tune. Notice the chord structure is the same as the first 8 measures, having modulated up a 5th from the key of Abmaj to the key of Ebmaj.

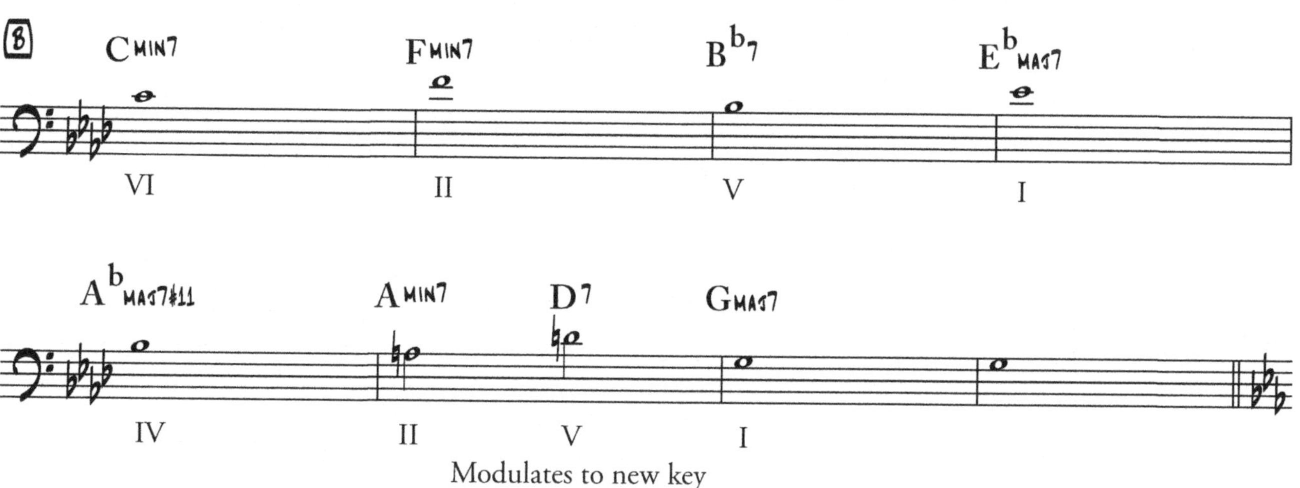

©Waterfall Publishing House 2012

Ex. 4 Diatonic 7ths in the key of Eb major

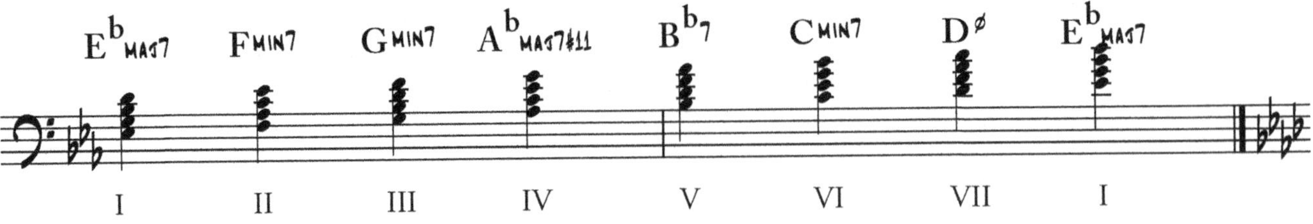

Ex. 5 shows the C section consisting of the II V I progression a minor third apart eg II V in G major modulating to II V in E major

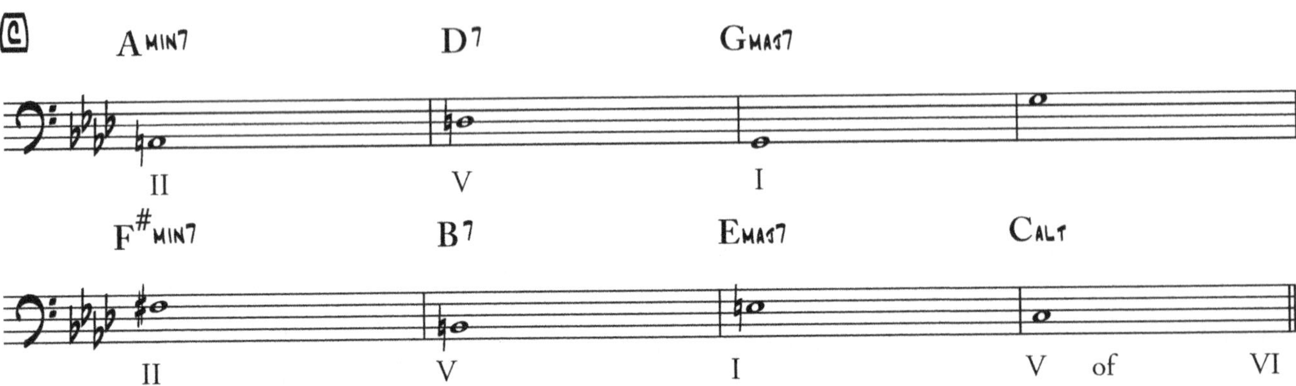

Ex. 6 shows the D section, the last 12 measures of the tune. The first 5 measures are the same as the A section. Notice from bar 5 the IV major to IV min bVII 7 progression. This variation is leading back to the top of the tune, notice the Cmin7 chord or the III min7 chord in the Key of Ab. The Cmin7 or III min7 is a substitute for the I chord.

From Cmin7 the progression is III VI II V I the last measure is the Minor II V leading back to the VI min7 chord at the top of the tune. The B diminished chord is used to create chromatic root movement instead of Fmin7 , outlining the III bIII II V I progression.

©Waterfall Publishing House 2012

Jazz standard chord progression # 5 in 12 keys

THE APPLICATION OF THE TURNAROUND INTO THE VI MINOR CHORD

©Waterfall Publishing House 2012

©Waterfall Publishing House 2012

©Waterfall Publishing House 2012

©Waterfall Publishing House 2012

©Waterfall Publishing House 2012

©Waterfall Publishing House 2012

©Waterfall Publishing House 2012

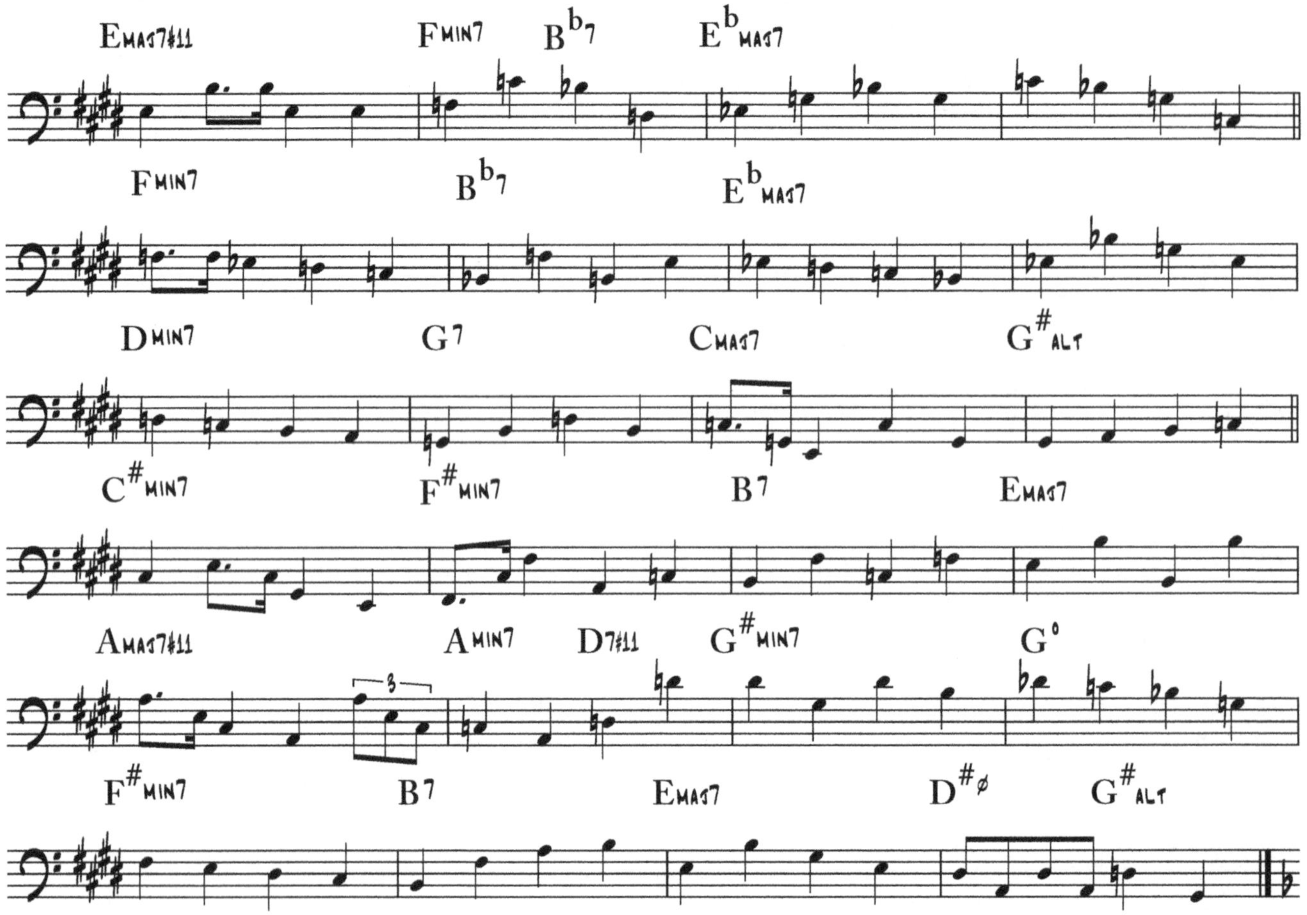
EMAJ7#11
FMIN7
Bb7
EbMAJ7
FMIN7
Bb7
EbMAJ7
DMIN7
G7
CMAJ7
G#ALT
C#MIN7
F#MIN7
B7
EMAJ7
AMAJ7#11
AMIN7
D7#11
G#MIN7
G°
F#MIN7
B7
EMAJ7
D#ø
G#ALT

F Major

DMIN7
GMIN7
C7
FMAJ7
BbMAJ#11
BMIN7
E7
AMAJ
AMIN7
DMIN7
G7
CMAJ7
FMAJ7#11
F#MIN7
B7
EMAJ7
F#MIN7
B7
EMAJ7

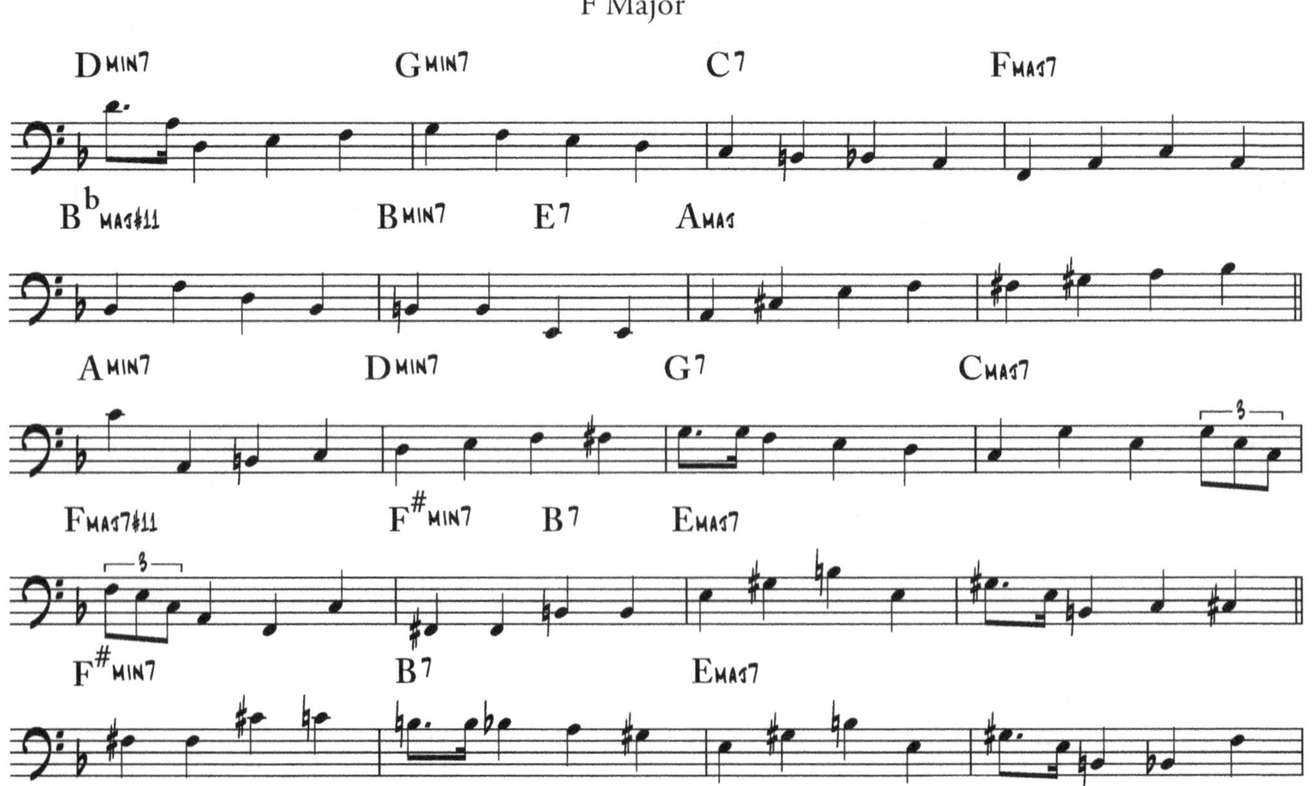

©Waterfall Publishing House 2012

©Waterfall Publishing House 2012

©Waterfall Publishing House 2012

Chapter 11

DIATONIC CHORD STRUCTURES & THE II V INTO THE IV CHORD BRIDGE

The diatonic chord structure outlined in this chapter is a classisc bebop chord progression played and practiced in all keys by the jazz masters.
The Form structure is AABA and 32 bars long.
The A section is a descending diatonic chord structure leading to the IV Dominant chord and then cycles back to the tonic via the V of V chord progression.
The second A has a variation in the last 4 bars due to the tune resolving before moving to the bridge.
The B section has the classic modulation of the II V into the IV major chord.
The last A section is essentially the same as the second A the tune resolves before modulating to the top of the tune.

The examples below show the digital analysis of the tune and the diatonic chord chart in the key of F major

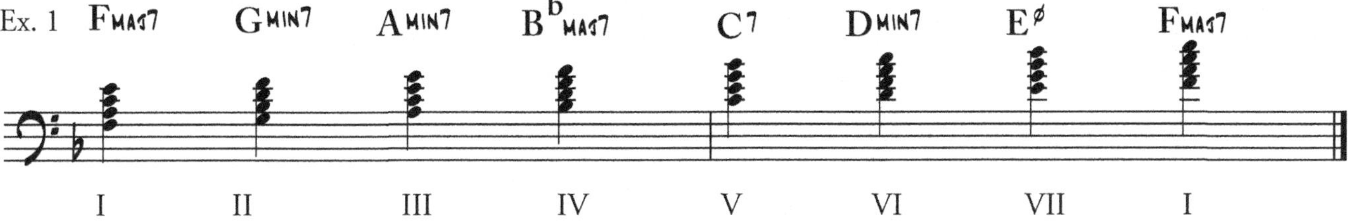

Ex. 2 Shows the 1st A section of jazz standard # 5

The example of the 1st A section shows the digital anaylsis of the chord structure, The chord sequence descends stepwise from Fmaj to the Bb7 chord in the 5th measure. Notice in the 4th bar Cmin7 F7 is a II V leading to the Bb7 chord the IV chord in the chord progression.
From the Bb 7 chord the progression then modulates back to the second A or Fmaj via the extended III VI II V progression in bars 6, 7& 8.
Bars 6, 7 & 8 outline the V of V cycle using the relative II min7 chord bars 6 & 8.

©Waterfall Publishing House 2012

Ex. 3

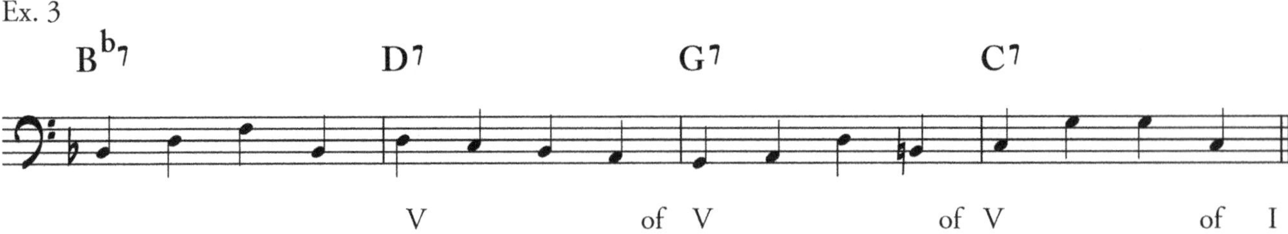

Ex. 3 shows measures 5 - 8 of the 1st A section outlining the V of V cycle, notice the Amin7 in bar 6 and Gmin7 in bar 8 have been omitted. From bar 6 we have the V of V cycle modulating to Fmaj. eg D is the 5th of G, G is the 5th of C, C is the 5th of Fmaj, the cycle is then resolved.

Ex. 4

Ex. 4 shows the V of V cycle using the relative II min 7 chords in bar 6 & 8 of the tune. The chord sequnce now has more of a bebop sound.The II V and the descending II V progressions are part of the bebop fundamentals for the jazz bassist. By understanding the chord structure and how the chords are functioning in any given tune enables the bassist to subsitute chords *on the fly* .

Ex. 5

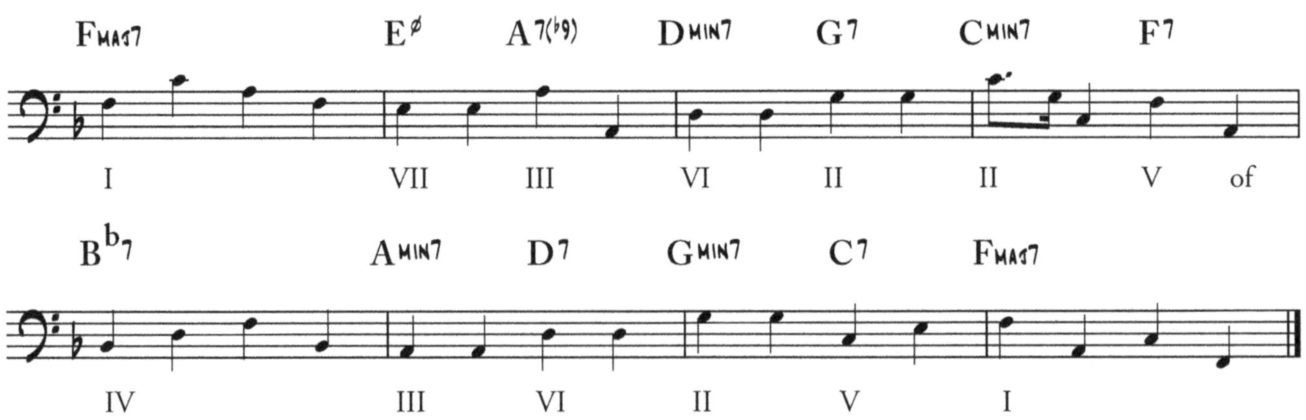

Ex. 5 shows the chord stucture of the 2nd A section, notice the variation in bars 6-8. the progression from bar 6 is now III VI II V I eg Amin7 D7 Gmin C7 - Fmaj7 . The progression now resolves in the last bar before moving to the B section

©Waterfall Publishing House 2012

Ex. 6 The Bridge & the II V into the IV major chord

Ex. 6 Shows the bridge of jazz standard # 5.
The bridge starts on the Cmin7 chord the II min7 chord leading to the Bbmaj chord. The first 4 bars of the B section are a II V into the IV chord. Bars 5 - 8 outline the II V in Dbmaj followed by a II V back to the tonic F maj.
The II V I in Db maj is a modulation of a minor third from Bb major.
The bridge then has a II V I in major a minor 3rd apart, eg II V in Bb major II V in Db major.
Looking at the root movement of the B section, the chord sequence modulates around the cycle of 4ths from C to Db then moves up a tritone to G, The II V leading to the tonic of the last A section Fmaj.

Ex. 7 Shows the Last A section of jazz standard # 5

Ex. 7 shows the chord stucture of the Last A section, notice that the 2nd A and Last A section have the same chord stucture, this is common in the AABA form of jazz standard chord progressions.

©Waterfall Publishing House 2012

Jazz standard chord progression # 6 in 12 keys

DIATONIC CHORD STRUCTURES & THE II V INTO THE IV CHORD BRIDGE

©Waterfall Publishing House 2012

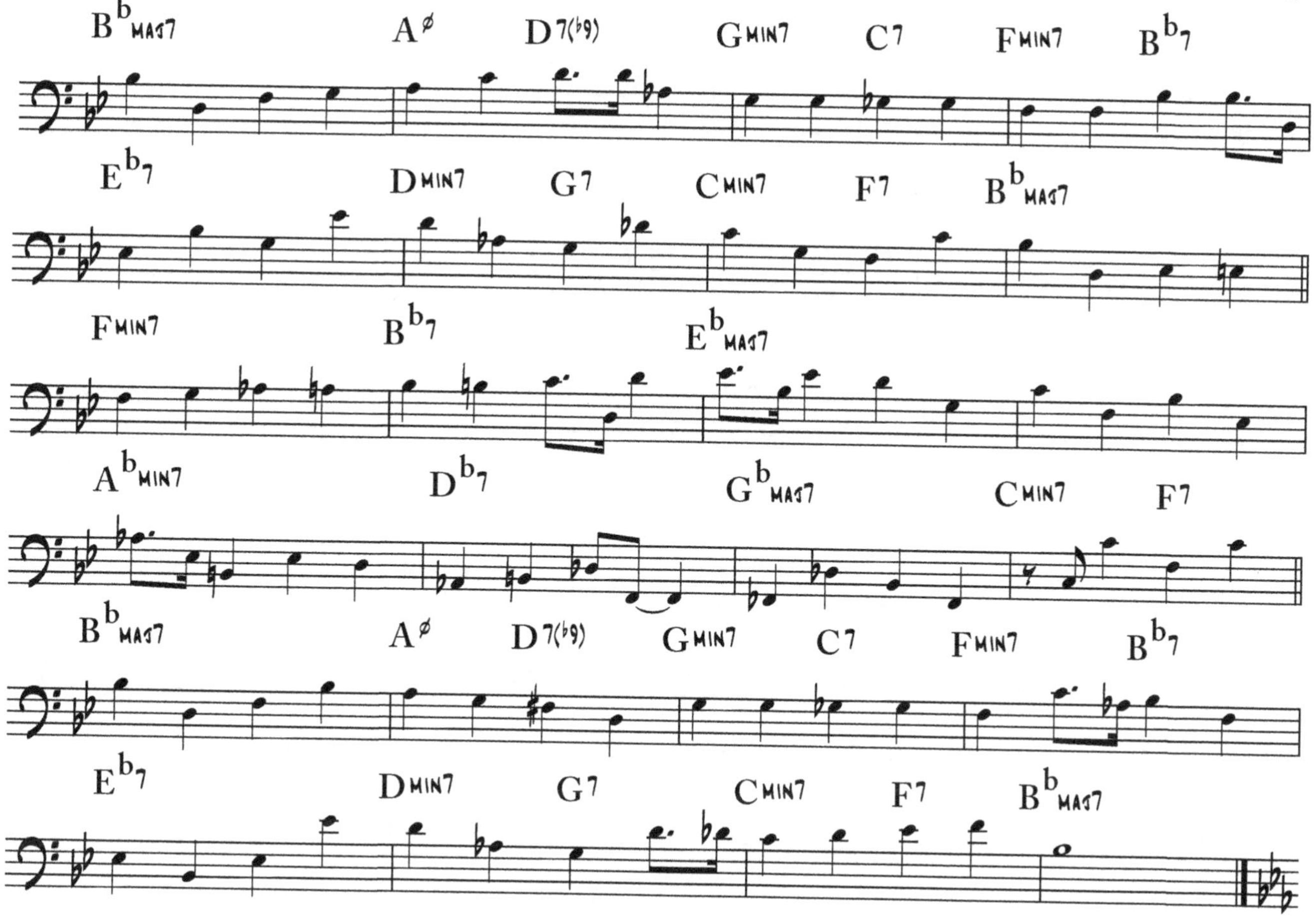
BbMAJ7 A∅ D7(b9) GMIN7 C7 FMIN7 Bb7
Eb7 DMIN7 G7 CMIN7 F7 BbMAJ7
FMIN7 Bb7 EbMAJ7
AbMIN7 Db7 GbMAJ7 CMIN7 F7
BbMAJ7 A∅ D7(b9) GMIN7 C7 FMIN7 Bb7
Eb7 DMIN7 G7 CMIN7 F7 BbMAJ7

Eb Major

EbMAJ7 D∅ G7(b9) CMIN7 F7 BbMIN7 Eb7
Ab7 GMIN7 C7 F7 FMIN7 Bb7
EbMAJ7 D∅ G7(b9) CMIN7 F7 BbMIN7 Eb7
3
Ab7 GMIN7 C7 FMIN7 Bb7 EbMAJ7
BbMIN7 Eb7 AbMAJ7

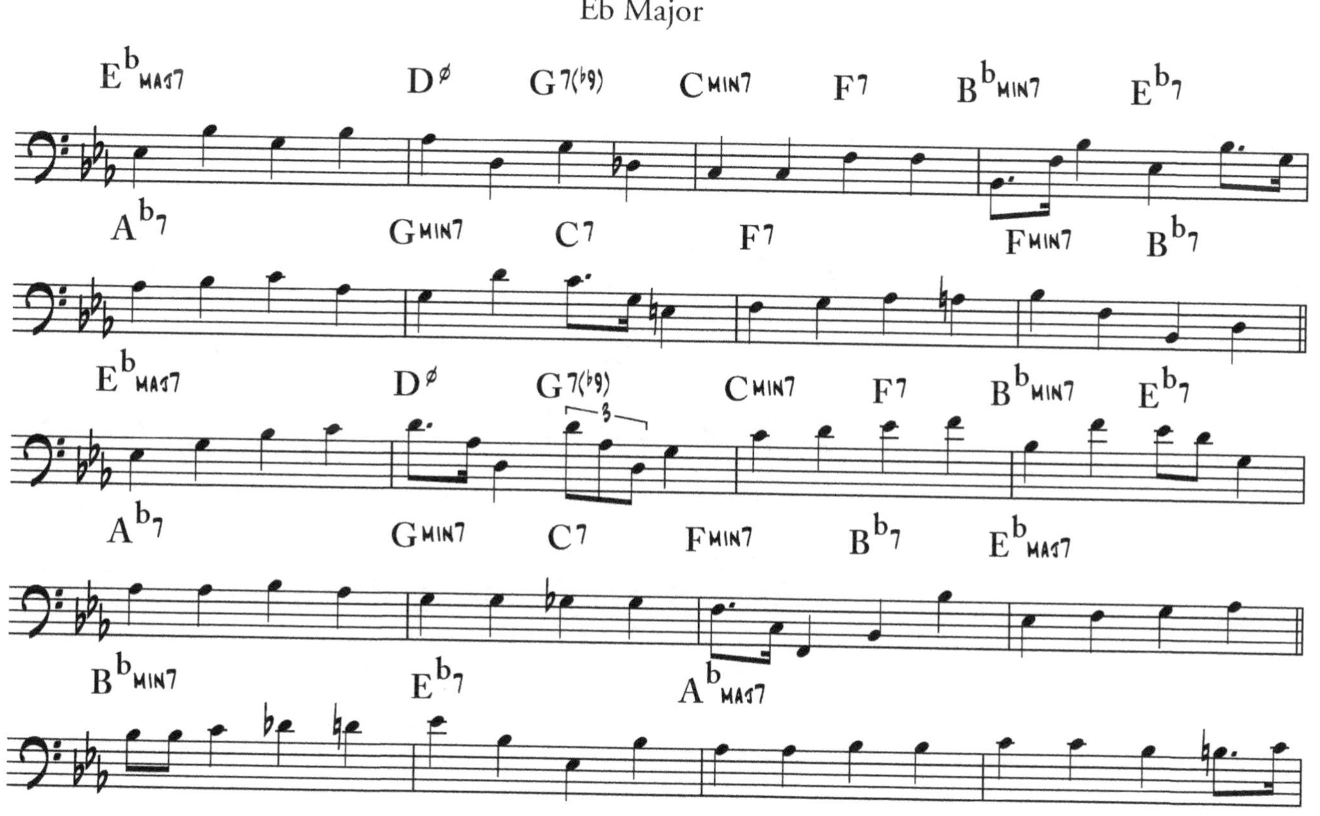

©Waterfall Publishing House 2012

©Waterfall Publishing House 2012

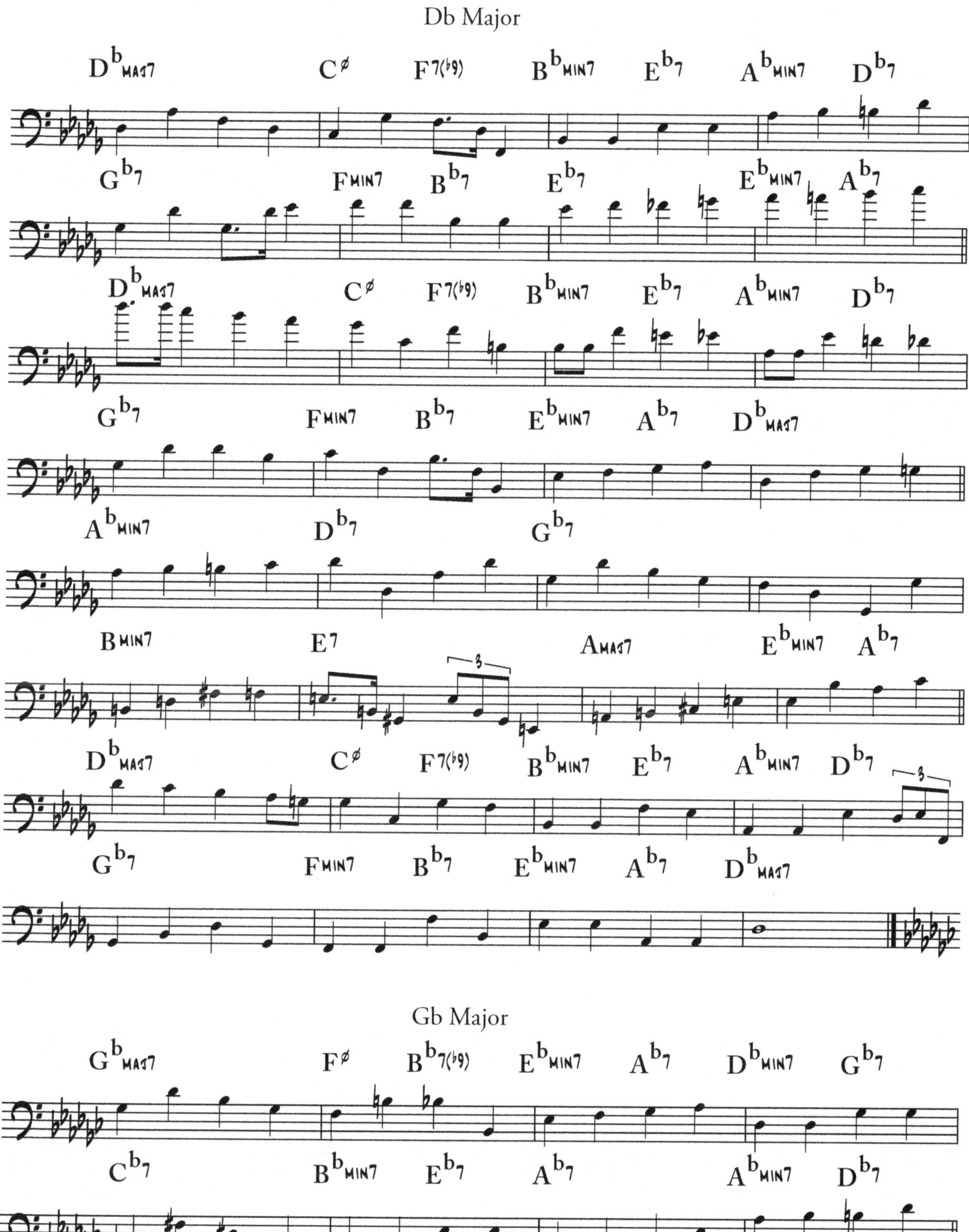

©Waterfall Publishing House 2012

©Waterfall Publishing House 2012

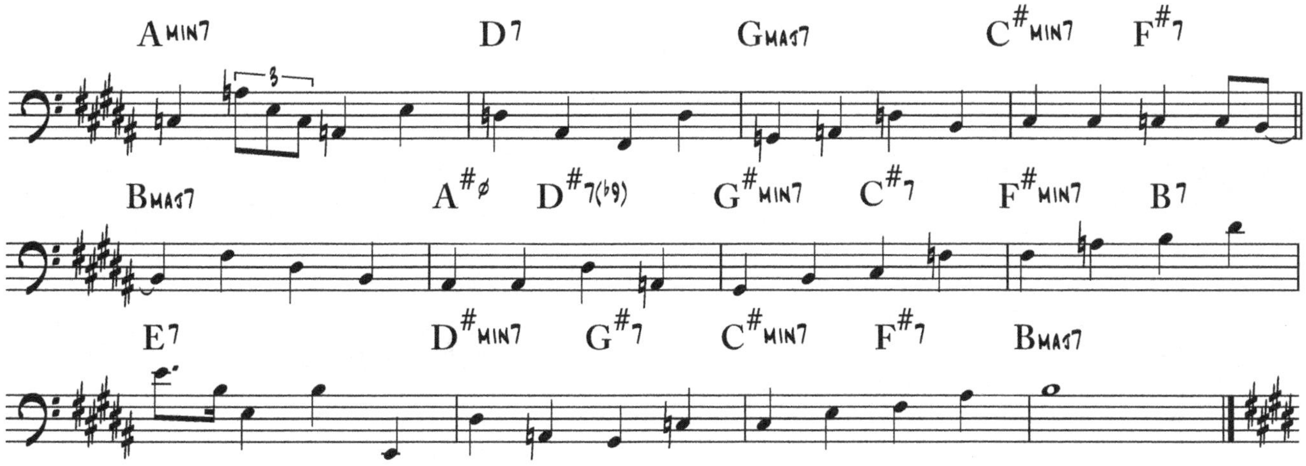
AMIN7 D7 GMAJ7 C#MIN7 F#7
BMAJ7 A#ø D#7(b9) G#MIN7 C#7 F#MIN7 B7
E7 D#MIN7 G#7 C#MIN7 F#7 BMAJ7

E Major

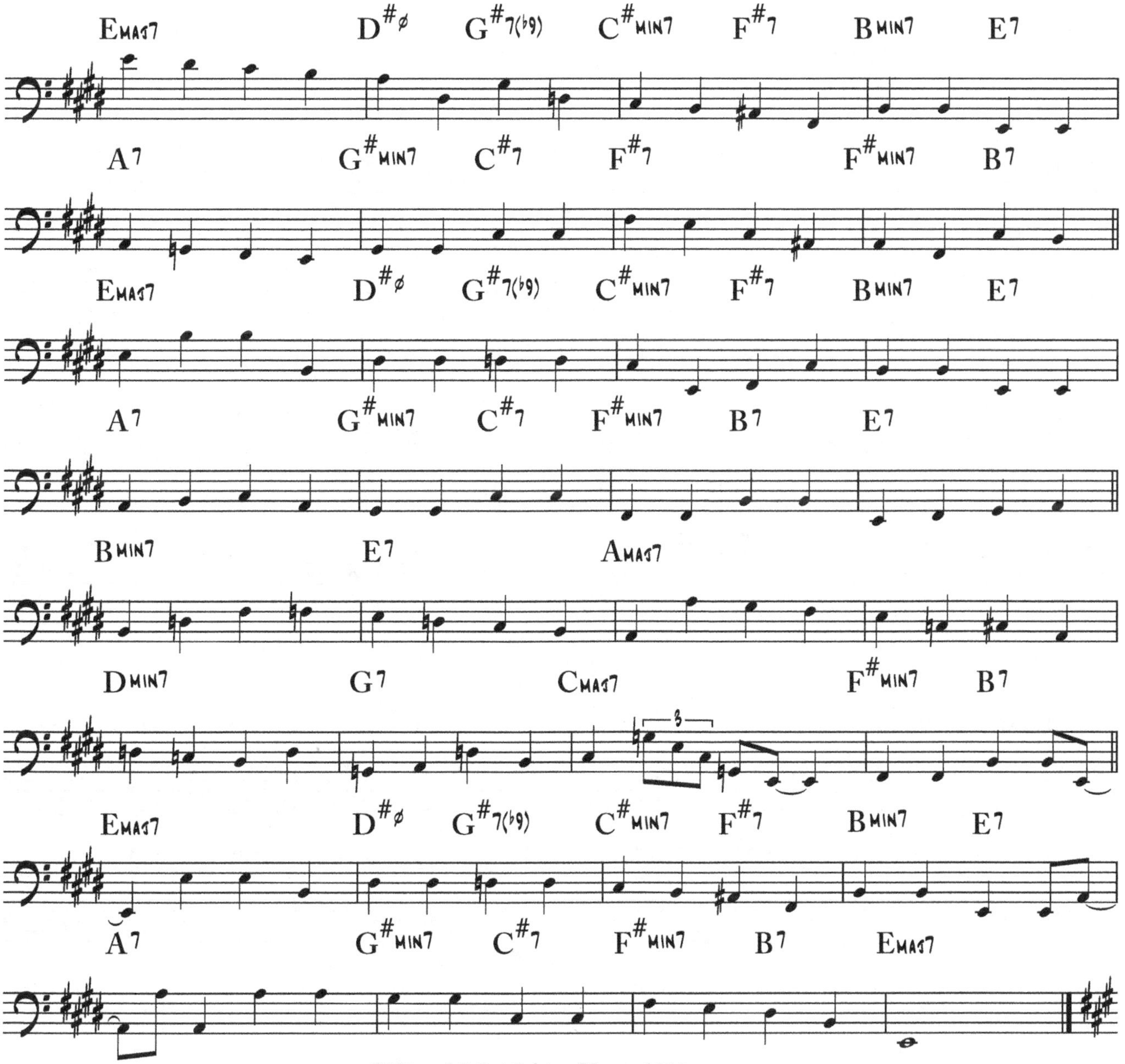

EMAJ7 D#ø G#7(b9) C#MIN7 F#7 BMIN7 E7
A7 G#MIN7 C#7 F#7 F#MIN7 B7
EMAJ7 D#ø G#7(b9) C#MIN7 F#7 BMIN7 E7
A7 G#MIN7 C#7 F#MIN7 B7 E7
BMIN7 E7 AMAJ7
DMIN7 G7 CMAJ7 F#MIN7 B7
EMAJ7 D#ø G#7(b9) C#MIN7 F#7 BMIN7 E7
A7 G#MIN7 C#7 F#MIN7 B7 EMAJ7

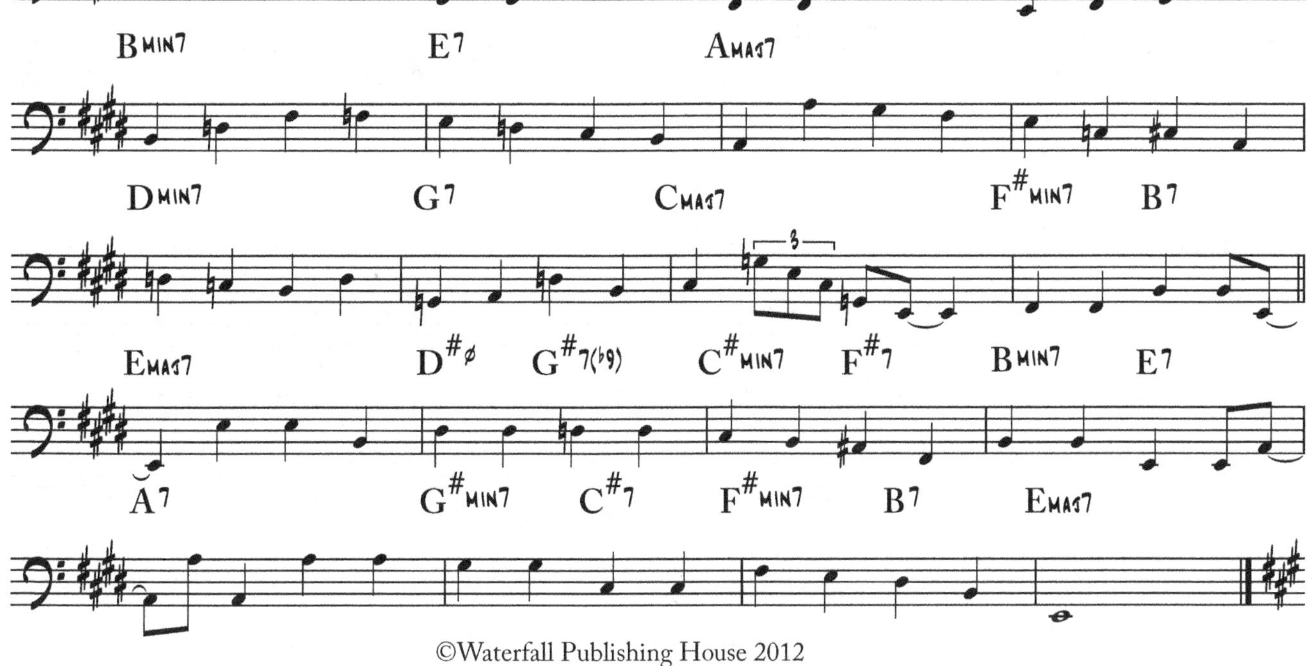

©Waterfall Publishing House 2012

©Waterfall Publishing House 2012

©Waterfall Publishing House 2012

©Waterfall Publishing House 2012

Chapter 12

TRITONE SUBSTITUTION IN 12 KEYS

The term tri tone substitute refers to a commonly used chord substitution used on the Dominant 7th chord in a II V progression or in a V of V progression.
The term tritone comes from the root notes being 3 whole steps or 3 tones apart, the distance between the tritone interval is also 3 tones or 3 whole steps.
The tritone substitute is often used to increase the harmonic rhtyhm eg more chords per bar and to create chromatic root movement.
Tritone substitution can also be used to create different chord tensions against the melody note.

Ex 1 shows the diatonic 7ths chart in the key of Bb major and the relationship of the V chord F7 .
The first examples of tritone substitution will be related to F7 and the tritone substitute B7.
All examples will then be shown in all 12 keys.

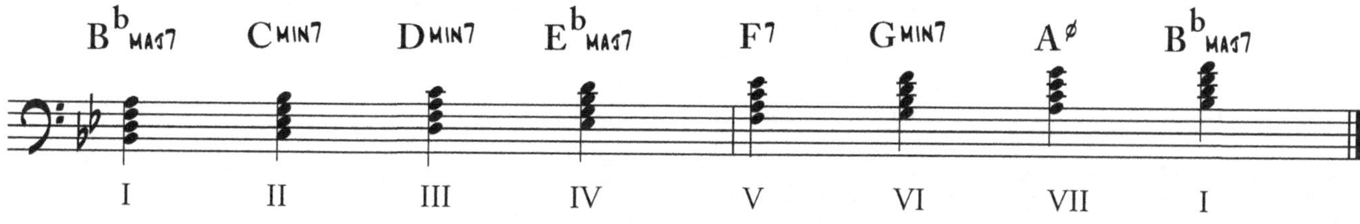

Ex. 2 shows the F7 arpeggio and the related tritone substitute B7
Note that the F7 and B7 chord have the same notes for the third and 7th

Ex. 3 shows the F chromatic scale and outlines the 3 whole steps between the root notes of the tritone substitutes and the tritone interval.

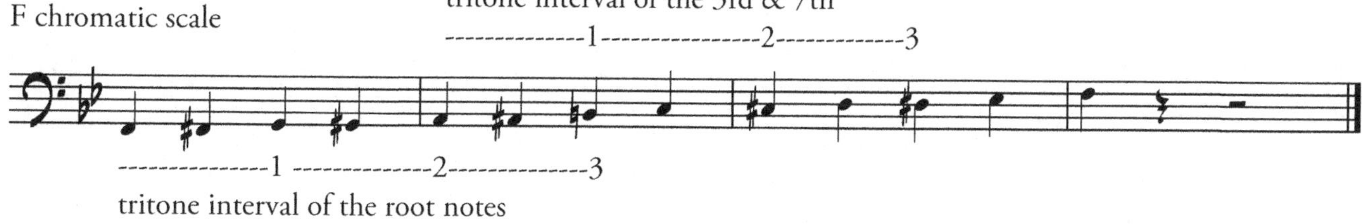

* Tri tone substitution has also been discussed in Constructing Walking Jazz Bass Lines book I & II, in this edition book IV the concept is taken and developed through all keys.

©Waterfall Publishing House 2012

Ex. 4 shows the IIV I progression in the key of Bb major

Ex. 5 shows the II V I in the key of Bb major with the F7 chord being substituted with the B7 chord. The root movement is now II bII I

Ex. 6 shows the the tritone substitute B7 using the relative II min7 F#min7. The progression now has greater harmonic rhythm.

Ex. 7 shows the original II V progression Cmin7 F7 followed by the Tritone substitution II V F#min7 B7. Now the harmonic rhythm has increased again. This progression is typical of the bebop era and how they approached standard chord changes.

Ex. 8 shows the tritone substitution F#min7 B7 surrounded by the original II V progression Cmin7 F7.

©Waterfall Publishing House 2012

TRITONE SUBSTITUTE CHORD PROGRESSIONS IN 12 KEYS

B Major

©Waterfall Publishing House 2012

©Waterfall Publishing House 2012

©Waterfall Publishing House 2012

©Waterfall Publishing House 2012

©Waterfall Publishing House 2012

©Waterfall Publishing House 2012

EXAMPLES OF TRITONE SUBSTITUTION APPLIED TO THE BRIDGE OF JAZZ STANDARD CHORD PROGRESSION # 7

The following examples show some of the possible tri tone chord substitutions available when playing over the Bridge or B section of Jazz standard # 7.
When using the tri tone substitutions it is a good idea to establish the sound or tonality of the tune before altering the harmony. For example on the melody or opening chorus of the solo it is a good idea to play the standard changes. This allows the soloist time to hear the harmonic progressions of the tune before suggesting any alterations.
Chord substitutions should be used to enhance the overall ensemble sound and to inspire the soloist, if youre playing behind someone who doesnt hear the substitutions dont play them. Inspire them by playing strong fundamental lines with good intonation and hard swinging time.
Some of the greatest jazz bassists can lay it down simply by playing roots and 5ths and horn players will be lined up down the block waiting for a chance to sit in.

Ex.1 Outlines the standard changes to the Bridge of Jazz standard # 7
Notice the II V I progression descending by whole step. The last chord the F7 leads back to the top of the last A.

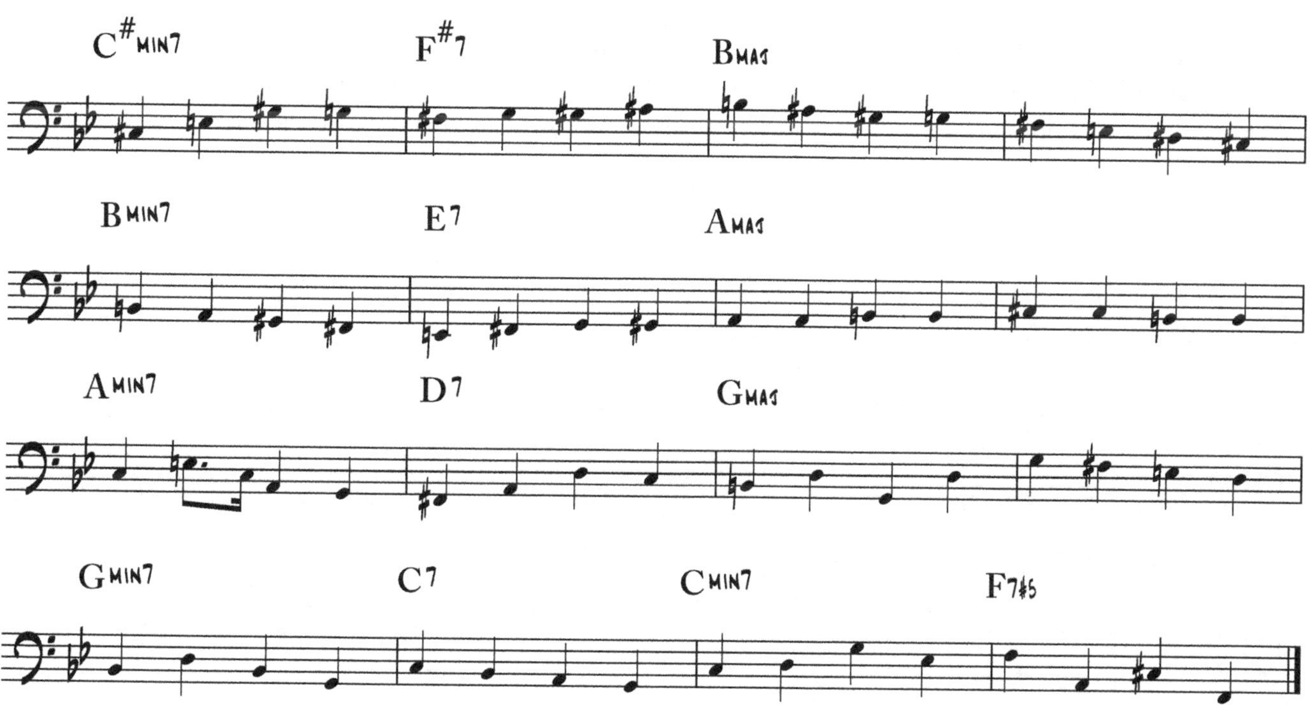

©Waterfall Publishing House 2012

Ex. 2 Outlines the tritone substitution in the 2nd measure of the II V I progression.
Notice the progression uses the relative II min7 of the tritone sustitute.

Ex. 3 Outlines the use of greater harmonic rhythm, eg two chords per bar.
Notice that the progression now has the original II V followed by the tri tone substitution.
Measures 13 - 14 outlines the tri tone substitution surrounded by the original II V progression.

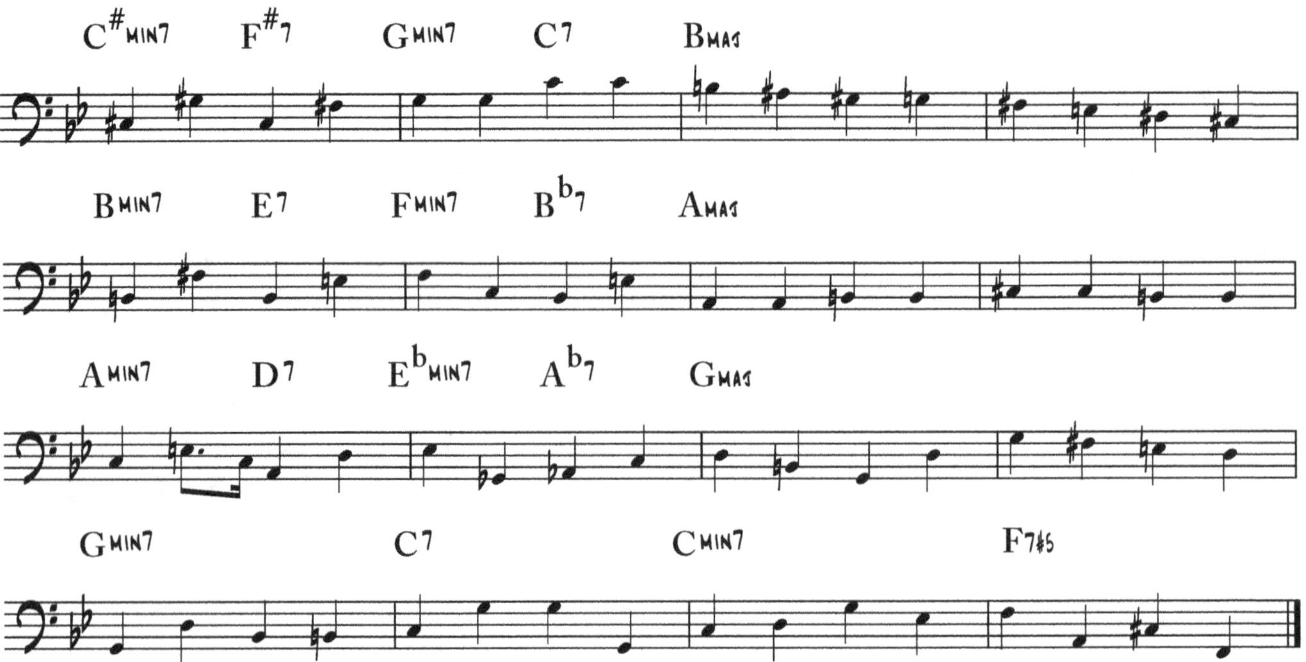

©Waterfall Publishing House 2012

Jazz standard chord progression # 7

THE APPLICATION OF TRI TONE SUBSTITUTION IN 12 KEYS

The use of tri tone substitutes outlined in the previous examples are applied to Jazz chord progression # 7. Notice that the tritone substitutes are applied to the A section as well as the B section and applied to all 12 keys. Each key outlines 2 choruses of walking bass line examples.

©Waterfall Publishing House 2012

©Waterfall Publishing House 2012

©Waterfall Publishing House 2012

B Major

©Waterfall Publishing House 2012

©Waterfall Publishing House 2012

©Waterfall Publishing House 2012

©Waterfall Publishing House 2012

©Waterfall Publishing House 2012

©Waterfall Publishing House 2012

©Waterfall Publishing House 2012

©Waterfall Publishing House 2012

©Waterfall Publishing House 2012

©Waterfall Publishing House 2012

©Waterfall Publishing House 2012

Eb Major

©Waterfall Publishing House 2012

©Waterfall Publishing House 2012

©Waterfall Publishing House 2012

©Waterfall Publishing House 2012

©Waterfall Publishing House 2012

©Waterfall Publishing House 2012

©Waterfall Publishing House 2012

©Waterfall Publishing House 2012

©Waterfall Publishing House 2012

©Waterfall Publishing House 2012

©Waterfall Publishing House 2012

G Major

©Waterfall Publishing House 2012

©Waterfall Publishing House 2012

©Waterfall Publishing House 2012

©Waterfall Publishing House 2012

©Waterfall Publishing House 2012

©Waterfall Publishing House 2012

©Waterfall Publishing House 2012

©Waterfall Publishing House 2012

©Waterfall Publishing House 2012

Chapter 13

ACCENTS, PHRASING AND ANTICIPATING THE CHORD CHANGES

Jazz standard chord progression # 8 is a 36 measure tune consisting of the ABA form.
The A section is 14 bars, the B section is 8 bars.
This particular tune is challenging to play due to the irregular structure, especially when trading with the drums. Concentration is the key.

In this chapter the concept of playing ahead of the bar or anticipating the chord changes will be covered as well as using rhythmic motifs, or sequences.
By using a rhythmic pattern or sequnce of repeated intervals the bass player can highlight or anchor a specific part of the tune, adding stability to the ensemble sound.
This enables the soloist to build momentum and really stretch out on what can easily become a difficult song form to play on.

Ex. 1 shows the B section of jazz standard # 8 an excerpt taken from the first chorus in the key of D major, notice in bars 5 -7 the rhythmic motif or sequence. In this example the rhythmic figure and intervals used are the same and descend by a half step through the chord changes.

Ex. 2 shows the B section of jazz standard # 8 an excerpt taken from the first chorus in the key of Eb major, notice in bars 5 -7 the sequence is used, this time using the triad eg 1 5 3 1. On the 4 and beat of the measure the chord change is anticipated and tied across the bar. This is an example of rhythmic phrasing and anticipating the chord changes.
Using these devices really makes the band swing and connects the bassist to the way the drummer may play the ride pattern.

©Waterfall Publishing House 2012

Phrasing is a personal touch and is one device that bassists use to identify their own sound. Listen to the classic recordings and transcribe some bass lines, you will notice that the lines or note choices are very similar amongst the giants.
What makes the line sound different is the players personality and own life experiences shining through into the music.
This is the true magic of jazz, each person has their own unique style and something to contribute.
As a starting point when first using this device try anticipating or playing into the 1 on the 4th bar or 8th bar of the form.
Playing into the 1 is often done as the sections change, eg going from the A section to the B section etc.
Again, these are examples there are no "*rules* ".

Jazz standard chord progression # 8 in 12 keys

APPLYING ACCENTS, PHRASING AND ANTICIPATING THE CHORD CHANGES IN 12 KEYS

Db Major

EMIN7 A7 EbMIN7 Ab7 DbMAJ CALT
AbMIN7 Db7 GbMAJ Gø C7(b9)
FMIN7 BbALT EbMIN7 AbALT
DbMAJ FMIN7 F#7#11
GALT CALT B7 Bb7
A7 Ab7 EMIN7 A7 EbMIN7 Ab7
DbMAJ CALT AbMIN7 Db7

©Waterfall Publishing House 2012

©Waterfall Publishing House 2012

D Major

©Waterfall Publishing House 2012

©Waterfall Publishing House 2012

©Waterfall Publishing House 2012

©Waterfall Publishing House 2012

©Waterfall Publishing House 2012

©Waterfall Publishing House 2012

©Waterfall Publishing House 2012

©Waterfall Publishing House 2012

G Major

©Waterfall Publishing House 2012

©Waterfall Publishing House 2012

©Waterfall Publishing House 2012

©Waterfall Publishing House 2012

©Waterfall Publishing House 2012

©Waterfall Publishing House 2012

©Waterfall Publishing House 2012

©Waterfall Publishing House 2012

C Major

©Waterfall Publishing House 2012

©Waterfall Publishing House 2012

Chapter 14

THE MINOR KEY TONALITY AND THE MINOR II V I

The following chapter outlines the Minor II V progression in 12 keys using jazz standard # 9 as an example.

When playing over the Minor II V progression one thing to be considered is that unlike the Major II V progression, the chords used are not from the same key. As an example a II V I in F major would be Gmin7 C7 Fmaj7. These chords are all diatonic chords from the key of F major.
When playing over the Minor II V progression the relationship of the chords changes . The II V chords are from keys a minor third apart. The tonic minor key is a major third away from the V chords key.

The examples below outline the relationships of the chords and keys related to the Minor II V progression.

Ex. 1 The II V I in F Minor.
Note the tonic minor chord used is the minor maj7 chord, the minor 6/9 chord is also often used as a tonic minor sound.

Ex. 2 G min7b5 chord scale the G locrian #2 this scale is the 6th mode of the Bb melodic minor scale.

Ex. 3 C alt chord scale the C altered or diminished whole tone scale is the 7th mode of the Db melodic minor scale.

©Waterfall Publishing House 2012

Ex. 4 Fmin maj7 chord scale F melodic minor the tonic minor scale

FMINMAJ7 (F melodic minor scale)

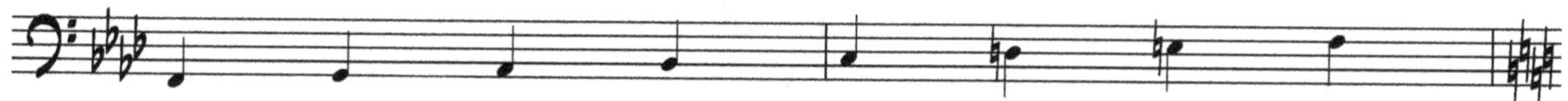

NB. The Minor II V and the uses of the Modes of the melodic minor scale has also been discussed in " Constructing Walking Jazz Bass Lines Book III - Standard Lines ".

THE MINOR II V PROGRESSION IN 12 KEYS

The examples shown below use the min/maj7 chord and the min6/9 chord as the tonic minor chord.

G∅ CALT FMINMAJ7

A♭∅ D♭ALT G♭MIN6/9

A∅ DALT GMINMAJ7

B♭∅ E♭ALT A♭MIN6/9

B∅ EALT AMINMAJ7

C∅ FALT B♭MIN6/9

C#∅ F#ALT BMINMAJ7

©Waterfall Publishing House 2012

Jazz standard chord progression # 9 in 12 keys

THE APPLICATION OF THE MINOR KEY TONALITY AND THE MINOR II V I IN 12 KEYS

©Waterfall Publishing House 2012

©Waterfall Publishing House 2012

G Minor

©Waterfall Publishing House 2012

©Waterfall Publishing House 2012

©Waterfall Publishing House 2012

©Waterfall Publishing House 2012

©Waterfall Publishing House 2012

©Waterfall Publishing House 2012

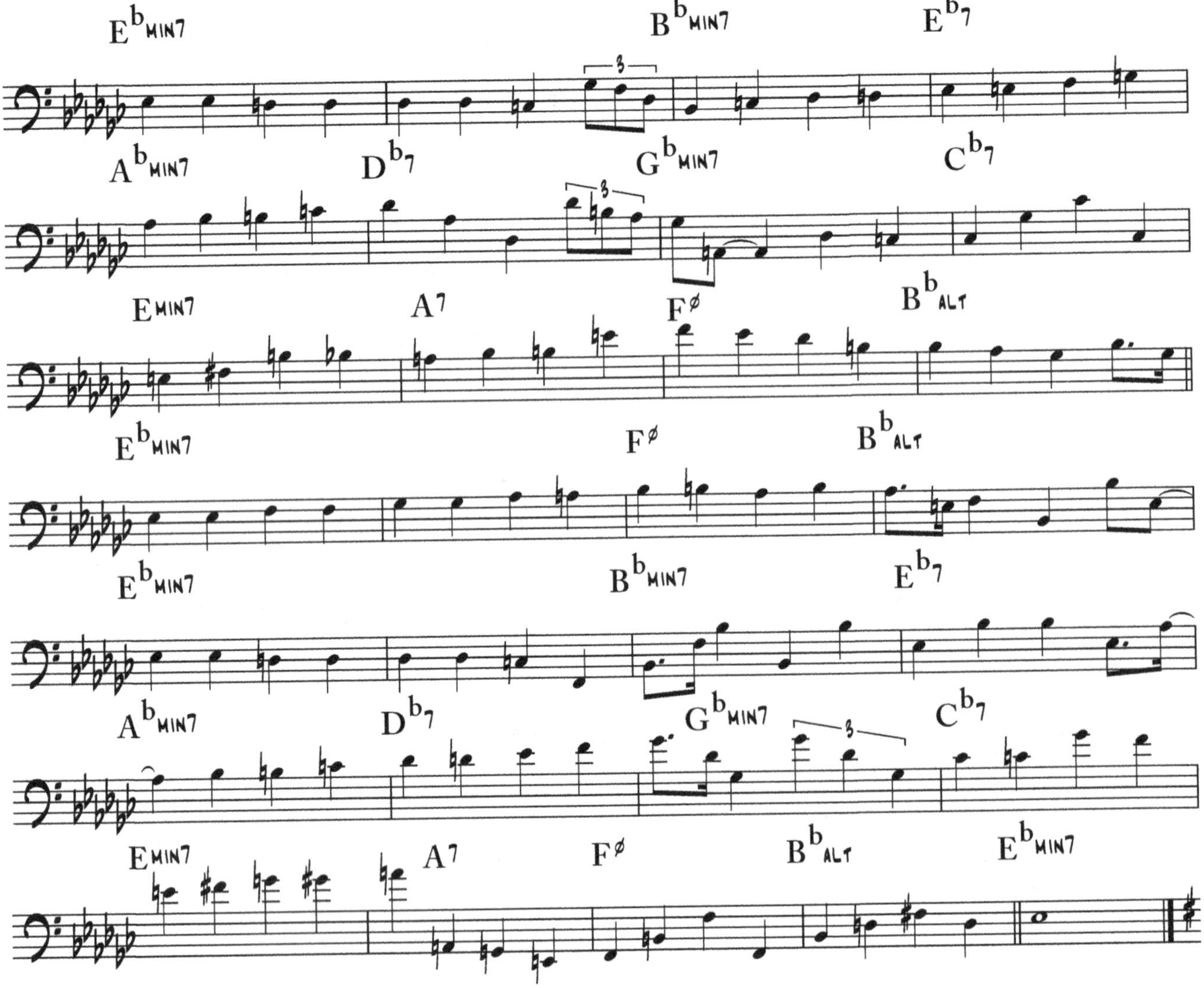

E♭MIN7 B♭MIN7 E♭7

A♭MIN7 D♭7 G♭MIN7 C♭7

EMIN7 A7 Fø B♭ALT

E♭MIN7 Fø B♭ALT

E♭MIN7 B♭MIN7 E♭7

A♭MIN7 D♭7 G♭MIN7 C♭7

EMIN7 A7 Fø B♭ALT E♭MIN7

E Minor

EMIN7 F♯ø BALT

EMIN7 BMIN7 E7

AMIN7 D7 GMIN7 C7

FMIN7 B♭7 F♯ø BALT

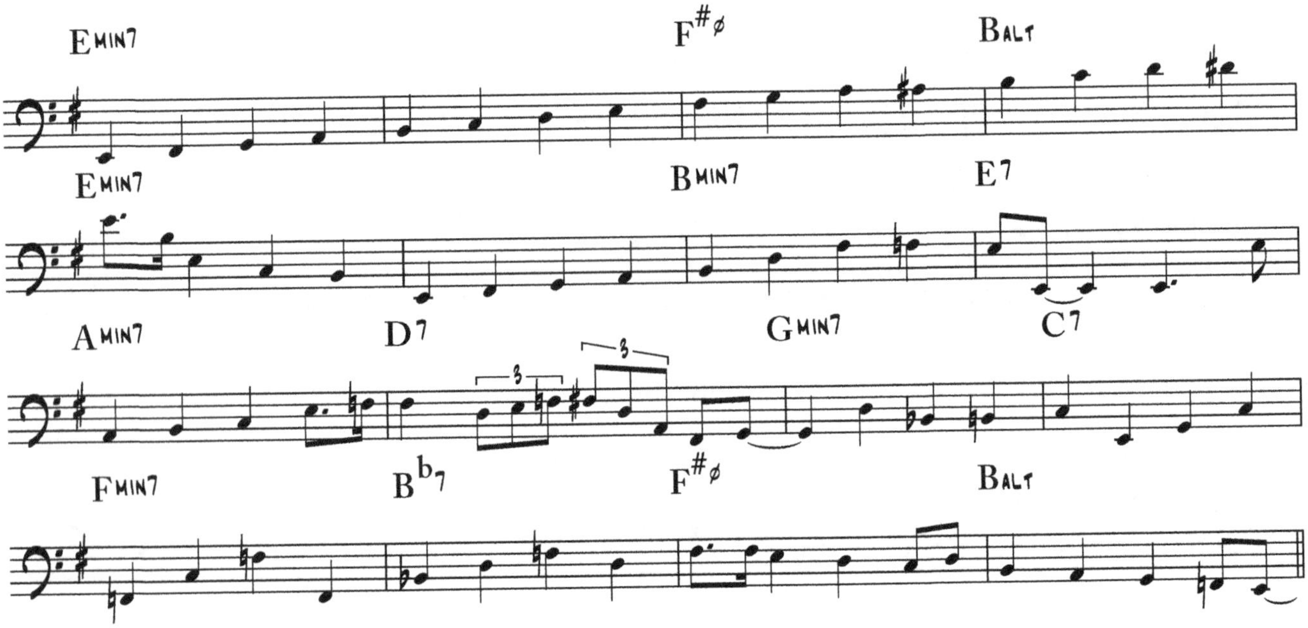

©Waterfall Publishing House 2012

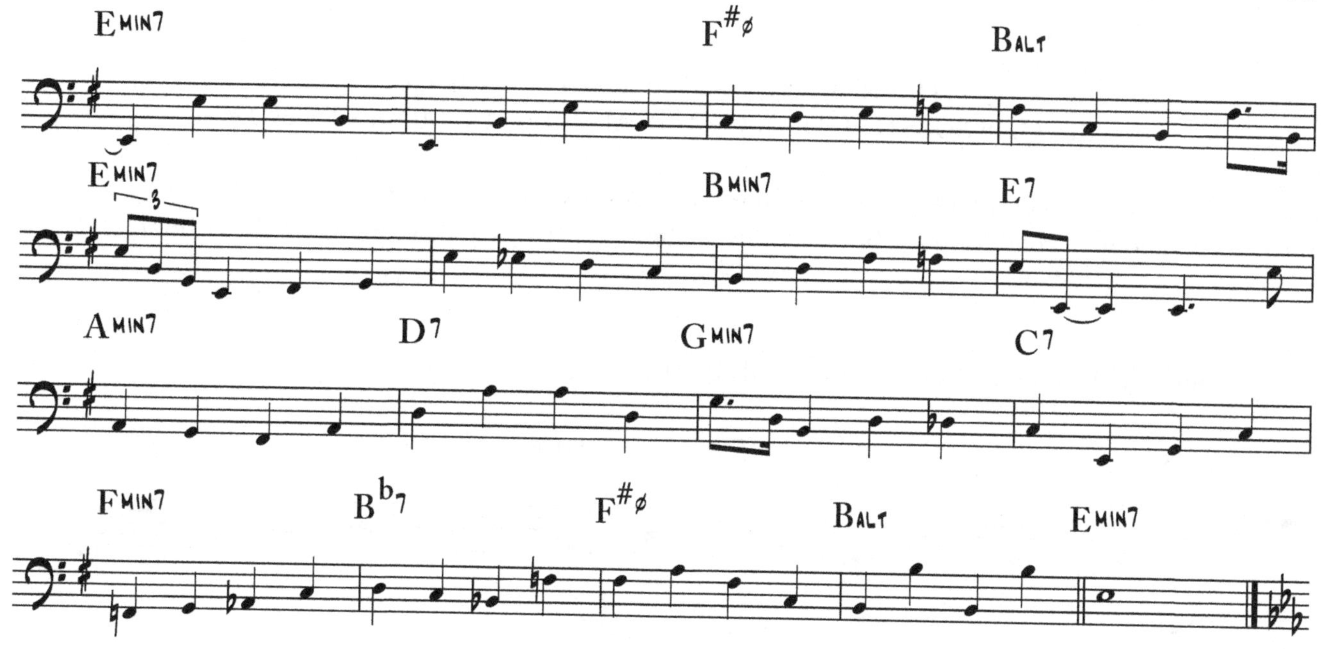

©Waterfall Publishing House 2012

Chapter 15

THE DESCENDING MINOR II V I BRIDGE .
TRI TONE SUBSTITUTION OF THE ALTERED DOMINANT CHORD

Jazz standard #10 uses the ABCD form with each section consisting of 16 measures.
The C section or often considered the Bridge in this progression consists of descending II V I in Minor.

Ex. 1 Outlines the 16 measure Bridge of jazz standard # 10

Ex. 2 Outlines the 16 measure Bridge of jazz standard # 10 after being reharmonized. These changes could be superimposed over the Bridge during the solos. When reharmonizing or substituting chords behind the melody be aware of the melody notes and the chord tones being played.

©Waterfall Publishing House 2012

Ex. 3 shows the 16 measure Bridge of jazz standard # 10 after being reharmonized. This time substituting the Altered Dominant chord for the Lydian Dominant chord.
Notice we now have chromatic root movement eg the first 4 measures of the bridge move chromatically C#, C, B.

F# Alt and C7#11 can be substituted because they are derived from the same scale G Melodic minor. Melodic minor harmony has no avoid notes, this means any chord from the scale can be substituted however this is more of a device used for soloing and not in a walking bass line context.
One thing to be considered when substituting chords as a bassist is, Am I adding to the music ?
Make choices based on where the music is going and who youre playing behind, sometimes the hardest swinging lines can be as simple as roots and fifths.
Remember the function of the bassist in a jazz setting eg bebop, hard bop etc is to lay down a solid foundation of time and harmony for the band.
This enables the soloist to build momentum and intensity.
Its also the key to getting hired.

Ex. 4 G Melodic minor

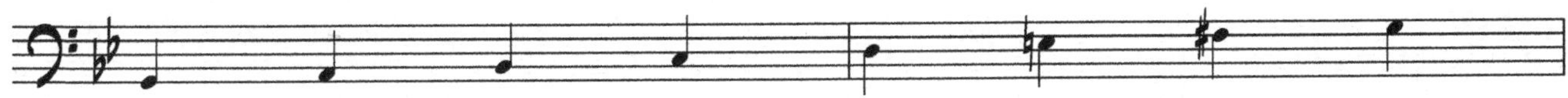

©Waterfall Publishing House 2012

Ex. 5 F# altered - G Melodic minor played from F# - F#

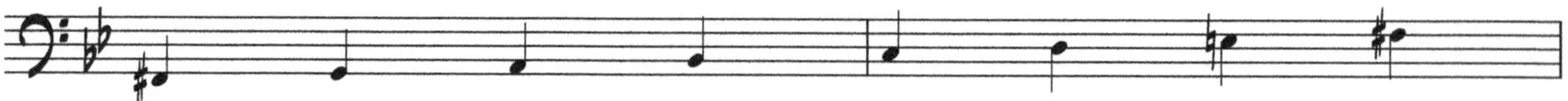

Ex. 6 C Lydian dominant - G Melodic minor played from C - C

Jazz standard chord progression # 10 in 12 keys

THE APPLICATION OF THE DESCENDING MINOR II V I BRIDGE
TRI TONE SUBSTITUTION OF THE ALTERED DOMINANT CHORD

Each key is outlined using 2 choruses of walking bass lines with the 2nd chorus using the reharmonization in the bridge, using either the Minor II V I or the tritone substitution of the Altered Dominant chord as outlined earlier in this chapter.

C Minor

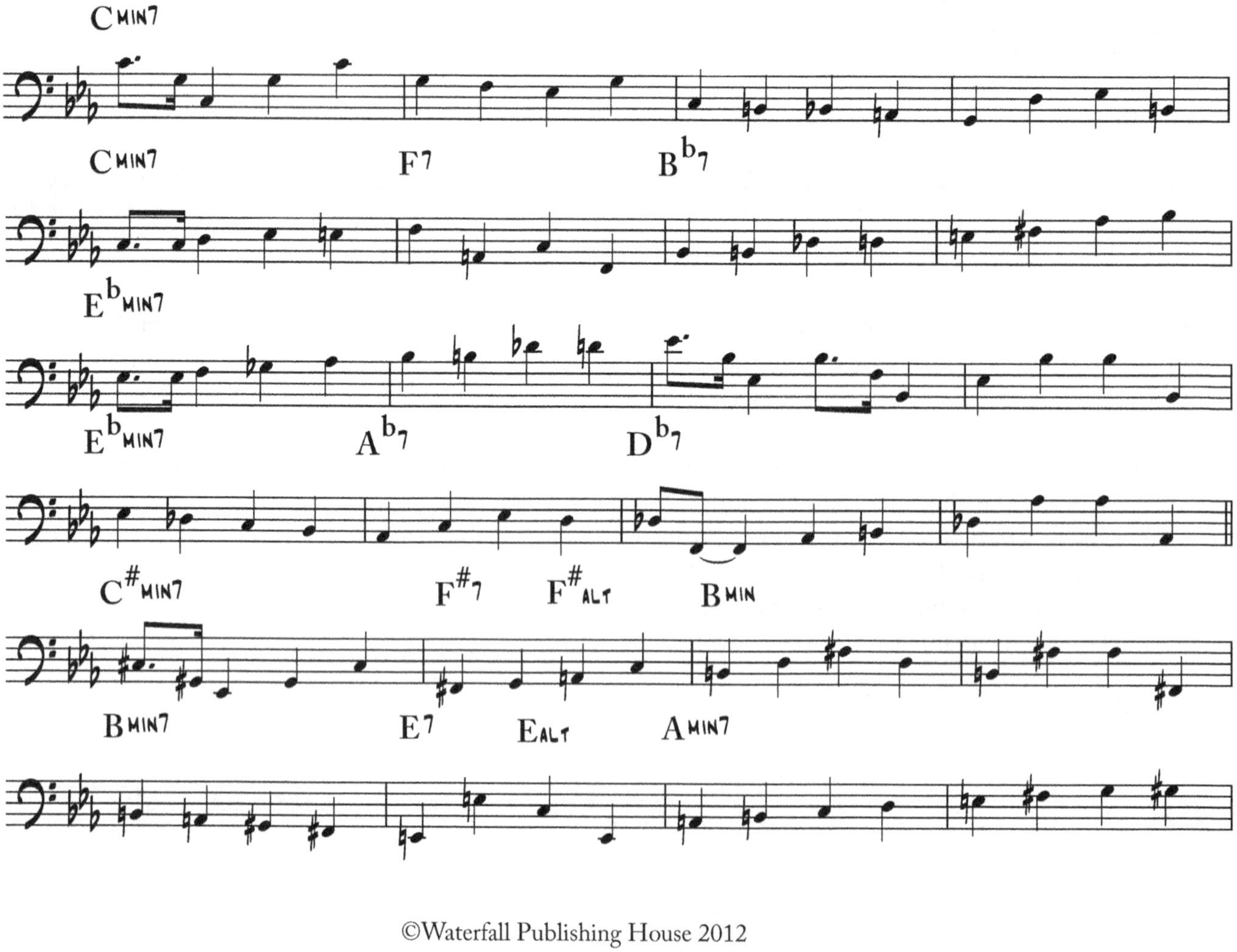

CMIN7

CMIN7 F7 Bb7

EbMIN7

EbMIN7 Ab7 Db7

C#MIN7 F#7 F#ALT BMIN

BMIN7 E7 EALT AMIN7

©Waterfall Publishing House 2012

©Waterfall Publishing House 2012

©Waterfall Publishing House 2012

©Waterfall Publishing House 2012

©Waterfall Publishing House 2012

D Minor

©Waterfall Publishing House 2012

©Waterfall Publishing House 2012

Eb Minor

©Waterfall Publishing House 2012

©Waterfall Publishing House 2012

©Waterfall Publishing House 2012

©Waterfall Publishing House 2012

©Waterfall Publishing House 2012

©Waterfall Publishing House 2012

©Waterfall Publishing House 2012

©Waterfall Publishing House 2012

©Waterfall Publishing House 2012

©Waterfall Publishing House 2012

©Waterfall Publishing House 2012

©Waterfall Publishing House 2012

Ab Minor

©Waterfall Publishing House 2012

©Waterfall Publishing House 2012

©Waterfall Publishing House 2012

©Waterfall Publishing House 2012

©Waterfall Publishing House 2012

©Waterfall Publishing House 2012

©Waterfall Publishing House 2012

©Waterfall Publishing House 2012

©Waterfall Publishing House 2012

IN CONCLUSION ......

It has been a vast amount of work and dedicated practice that brings the bassist to the last page of this book having covered all the examples within.

It has been the aim of this book to give the aspiring bassist a solid grounding in understanding how to construct walking jazz bass lines and support a melody and or soloist.

Having covered the material in this book you are now well on your way to finding your own voice as a bassist and as a jazz musician.
Listen to as much music as you can, Listen to the masters.

NB. This book is designed to make the student familiar with reading and understanding chord symbols in a jazz context, therefore the use of enharmonics is applied.

The objective has been to make the material for the student as easy to absorb as possible, as a confidance building mechanism.

Your thoughts and comments are important to us and assist us in providing future generations of musicians with quality educational material.

Please send youre thoughts or comments to constructwalkingjazzbasslines@gmail.com

©Waterfall Publishing House 2012

Other books available in this series

PRINT EDITIONS

" Constructing Walking Jazz Bass Lines " Book I
Walking Bass Lines : The Blues in 12 Keys

" Constructing Walking Jazz Bass Lines " Book II
Walking Bass Lines : Rhythm Changes in 12 keys

" Constructing Walking Jazz Bass Lines " Book III
Walking Bass Lines : Standard Lines

" Constructing Walking Jazz Bass Lines " Book IV
Building a 12 Key Facility for the Jazz Bassist Book I

" Constructing Walking Jazz Bass Lines " Book V
Building a 12 Key Facility for the Jazz Bassist Book II

Bass Tablature Series

" Constructing Walking Jazz Bass Lines " Book I
Walking Bass Lines : The Blues in 12 Keys -Bass TAB Edition

" Constructing Walking Jazz Bass Lines " Book II
Walking Bass Lines : Rhythm Changes in 12 Keys - Bass TAB Edition

" Constructing Walking Jazz Bass Lines " Book III
Walking Bass Lines : Standard Lines - Bass TAB Edition

" Constructing Walking Jazz Bass Lines " Book IV
Building a 12 Key Facility for the Jazz Bassist Book I - Bass Tab Edition

" Constructing Walking Jazz Bass Lines " Book V
Building a 12 Key Facility for the Jazz Bassist Book II - Bass Tab Edition

©Waterfall Publishing House 2012

E-BOOK EDITIONS

All books in the Constructing Walking Jazz Bass Lines series are also available as an eBook for the following reader formats Kindle, iTunes iBookstore, Nook, and Adobe Digital PDF. Follow us on the web for news and new release updates.

http://waterfallpublishinghouse.com

http://constructingwalkingjazzbasslines.com

http://basstab.net

Waterfall Publishing House is proud to be associated with the Trees for the Future Organisation. Visit them on the web at www.plant-trees.org .
Waterfall Publishing House will plant 1 tree per book sold in the " Constructing Walking Jazz Bass Lines " series through the " Trees for the Future " tree planting program and will match the commitment for a total of 2 trees planted per book sold.

Follow our quarterly progress at Waterfallpublishinghouse.com

©Waterfall Publishing House 2012

Made in the USA
Middletown, DE
01 February 2019